"Tell Me A Little Bit About Yourself"

Travis Hanson

authorHOUSE®

AuthorHouse™
1663 Liberty Drive
Bloomington, IN 47403
www.authorhouse.com
Phone: 1-800-839-8640

First published by AuthorHouse   01/06/2012

ISBN: 978-1-4685-3660-7 (sc)
ISBN: 978-1-4685-3659-1 (hc)
ISBN: 978-1-4685-4006-2 (ebk)

Library of Congress Control Number: 2012900103

Printed in the United States of America

Any people depicted in stock imagery provided by Thinkstock are models, and such images are being used for illustrative purposes only.
Certain stock imagery © Thinkstock.

This book is printed on acid-free paper.

Contents

All names have been changed to protect myself.

1

JOB INTERVIEWS SUCK. All of them. Even the ones that went well enough for me to land that sought after job that made me feel like a prostitute because I got paid to do stuff I didn't want to do and had to be friendly to people I didn't like. Those sucked too.

It's the whole process that makes me want to spit up. From the desperation, to the nervousness, to the forced conversations with a tool of a manager, to the anxiety of not knowing if you made a good enough first impression to get the job you really didn't want but need. I have been on a lot of interviews in my life and they all have been the same and have had those same ingredients. The last one I went on was no different and was just how I remembered them all to be.

First off, I already feel like a piece of feces because I haven't had anything to do in who knows how long, I have no money, no confidence, and everyone is constantly asking in a condescending way if I have found a job yet, like it's something I can just go pick up off the shelf at WalMart. On top of that, the hopelessness is starting to settle in because after spending the last couple of weeks walking into every restaurant, clothing store, office building, and any other building that would let me in, asking if they were hiring, I keep getting the same answer followed by, "We are always accepting applications though if you would like to fill one out." So I have filled out at least fifty seven of those damn things by now and turned my entire life history in for complete strangers to read, and still not one call.

I don't know what else to do at this point, it seems I have applied everywhere, so I decide to take a few days "off" from job hunting and regroup.

Neither the phone has rang nor has my butt left the couch in about three days now and I'm really starting to worry about myself and then one day I get woken up at the crack of noon by a phone call from the Abercrombie store informing me they are hiring a new shirt folder and they would like me to come in for an interview. My first instinct is to not show up because folding shirts for a living would almost be as bad as not doing anything for a living, but the whore in me comes out and thinks about the regular paycheck and I tell myself how it can't be that bad. So after arguing with myself for an hour and a half, I decide to put my pride aside and go meet this over enthusiastic manager named Todd who is really looking forward to meeting me.

So I get into the shower and try to scrub all the laying around on the couch watching decade old reruns of sitcoms funk off of me, shave the three day old stubble and Cheeto residue off my face, slap some Febreze on, and put on my least wrinkled button up shirt and the khakis I once wore to a wedding. I'm already feeling better about myself because I am wearing grown up clothes and have somewhere to be at a certain time and that's exciting. But as soon as I have managed to dress myself to the best of my abilities, I start panicking. I have to rehearse what I am going to say and how I am going to answer the in depth interview questions like, "Why should we hire you?" and "What is your definition of a team player?" and "Where do you see yourself in five years?" I don't want my answers to sound rehearsed but I do want to be able to talk myself up without sounding cocky or fake, so it's a delicate blend.

But the question that makes me panic the most though isn't even really a question. It's a 'put you on the spot so much that you have no idea how to respond' demand: "Tell me a little bit about yourself." I never know how to answer that. What do they want to know? I know they are looking more at how I answer it than what I actually say, but where do I begin? At the beginning or do I just tell them how much of a go getter I am and how much I like those little chocolate donuts from the grocery store? Do I keep it strictly work related or do I reveal some of my darkest secrets? What is appropriate to tell a complete stranger? In the past I have pretty much kept it short and sweet, probably too short because after I have stopped talking, they just stare at me waiting to see if that's all there really is to me. That has never really worked out too well for me so I think maybe I should change my tactics this time.

I still have some time before I have to be there, but I go fire up the car anyway because I'm getting antsy. If I'm early it will just give me more time to calm myself down and get familiar with the surroundings.

The closer I get to the interview, the more nervous I get and the baby blue shirt I'm wearing doesn't seem like such a good idea anymore because the dark blue sweat stains in my pits are growing by the second and they are impossible to hide. I crank the air conditioning up and the stereo down because I am almost there and for some reason I can't find where I'm going with the stereo on. The parking lot is empty but I find a parking spot about a half mile away from the entrance and sit in my car. I still have like forty five minutes before I have to go get interrogated, so I might as well go over my spontaneous answers again.

By now I have rehearsed my answers so much that they just sound stupid, so I decide to just wing it and I didn't want this stupid job anyway, and this will just be a practice interview for the next one I get. As I am sitting there in my car over thinking everything and looking at my watch every seventeen seconds, I start to feel that knot in my stomach forming and the nervous gas starts kicking in. Those nervous farts are impossible to control, but I have to try to get a handle on them, so I take one last look at myself in the rear view mirror to check for things hanging out of my nose, and get out of my car and try to walk the farts off. As I am walking and farting, I notice the first impression I am about to make. My baby blue shirt is now dark blue on both sides from my pits down to my belt from being soaking wet, my mouth is so dry from nerves I doubt I will be able to pronounce my name, my hands are profusely sweating even though they feel like I have kept them in the freezer for the last two hours, and my nervous farts are almost non stop, like my butt is trying to blow out a trick candle. Who wouldn't want to hire this?

So I get to the front door, take one last deep breath, and go to push the door open even though the sign says pull. Perfect. After I figure out how to open a door correctly, I am greeted by a very cute, outgoing young lady wearing Capri's who would like to know how she can help me. I muster up enough spit to ask for the manager and tell her I am here for an interview and I notice the instant change in attitude from her. She is now better than me. One more ego boost for me before I have to go talk myself up to some qualified stranger who will then decide if I am good enough to be part of their team and fold shirts for six dollars an hour. She goes to the back to get the manager and it seems to take forever. I know they aren't doing anything back there except talking about me and peeking around the corner at me so they can come out right as I am touching something I shouldn't be touching, but I wait patiently and awkwardly.

The young lady comes back out and tells me in a way that sounds like I have completely ruined her day, that Todd will be right out. She doesn't even look at me as she walks back to the register and gets back to her texting, so I just stand there feeling the material of the shirt on display in front of me pretending I don't notice the awkward silence. All of a sudden I hear my name and turn around to see this guy headed towards me at an incredibly quick pace. He is wearing black slacks and a khaki colored Abercrombie button up shirt with the sleeves rolled up. He seems to have missed a few of the top buttons though so you can see his unearned dog tags and his shoes are blindingly shiny and kind of pointy like exaggerated cowboy boots. His over the top enthusiasm is really projected through his wide eyes, giant smile, and pep in his step. He is overcompensating for something and has a special hair-do to prove it. This guy's name has got to be Todd.

"Hi I'm Todd, I'm the manager here. Good to meet you bro" as he crushes my hand and tells me to follow him back to his office so we can "chat". The smell of cologne in his office makes me want to gag and so does the thought of him becoming my boss. His office is decorated with all kinds of motivational posters and all of the pictures on his desk are of him being sporty. There are also stacks of paperwork all over which leads him into making some stupid joke about how messy his office is and I laugh really loud like it was funny. Then the silence makes it feel like I have to say something, so I try to form a bond with him and tell him how messy my bedroom is and how I have clothes all over the place. Oops, shouldn't have said that, I am here to get hired to neatly fold shirts and put them away. That is all the job requires and I have already in the first minute, expressed how I am not qualified to do that. The interview hasn't even officially started yet. I should just thank him for his time and leave now, but he chuckles in a staged way and leans way back in his chair and puts his hands together on top of his head showing me that this is just a casual conversation with one of the guys.

He starts in by talking about himself. Shocker. I try really hard to listen as he talks about what a great boss he is and his open door policy, but I find it very difficult to listen to him when all I can listen to is myself staring at his controlled chaos of a hair-do and the five o'clock shadow on his chest. His hair appears so messy and unkept, yet it is so perfect.

After he gets done telling me how successful he has become, he starts explaining what the shirt folding job entails. Pretty much just folding shirts, but he makes it sound so much more detailed and challenging that I actually doubt if I am smart enough to do the job. After a few more agonizing minutes of learning about Todd, the job, and the company and what it can do for me, should I be honored enough to become the newest team member, he starts the interrogation process by nonchalantly asking me one of the questions I expected I would be asked, "What made you come in and apply with us today?"

What I want to say is, "Desperation." but that's probably not the best answer, so instead of telling the truth and explaining how I don't even really remember applying here and how I don't care where I get hired as long as it's someplace that gives me a paycheck, I lie and tell him how big of a fan I am of Abercrombie's clothes and accessories and how "every time" I come into the store I notice how knowledgeable and friendly all of the employees are and how happy they look and how much I would like to be part of that. I add on how I really enjoy helping people and how eager I am to learn something new and how much of a quick learner I am, etc., etc.

As I am regurgitating these cliches that I would never say in my real life, I can't help but notice how exaggerated Todd's expressions are while he is listening to me. Leaning much too forward in his seat with that intense interested look, eyes that are focused in on me like every word I say is the most fascinating thing he has ever heard, and the reassuring head bob that let's me know he is really understanding what I am saying. This guy's a tool.

I finish reciting my lines and it appears I have just blown him away because his smile gets bigger and he just stares at me and says, "Excellent." like I'm a retarded eight year old who just tied his shoes for the first time. I hate this guy.

As he picks up my application and pretends to look it over for a third time, I wonder what his next question will be. Will he want to know if I am a team player? Will I have to explain why he should hire me over the other applicants? I hope so since I'm prepared and have memorized my lines for those responses. As long as he doesn't ask me to 'tell him a little bit about myself'. That one I am not prepared for. I don't like talking about myself and I never know how to answer that. Please don't ask me that.

He sets down my application, leans back, crosses one leg over the other and says, "Tell me a little bit about yourself Travis." So I do.

"My name is Travis Hanson, I'm thirty five years old and I was born December 19, 1975 in Butte, Montana. My mom had moved there to go to school to become a veterinarian and had met my dad, they got married and had me. They got divorced a couple of years later and my mom loaded me and our German Shepard Chauncy up in the car and drove back to Reno where she was from and where her side of the family still lived. We moved in with my aunt until my mom could save up enough to get our own place. My dad wasn't paying much, if any, child support and it wasn't easy for my mom to save, so we stayed there for a while, which was fine with me since I had my own room. I really don't remember any of this, being that I was only about two years old or so, but it's what I have been told. I will however, never forget my first memory.

It was shortly after we had moved in with my aunt, I'm not sure exactly how old I was but I think I was two or three. I was in my room playing with my toys, I had a lot of toys and they were the good ones too because I was the only child in the family and my grandma and grandpa were happy that their only grandchild now lived in the same city. So I was playing and I heard yelling coming from the front room and then all of a sudden some man with a mustache comes into my room, scoops me up in his arm, grabs my superhero sleeping bag, and starts heading towards the front door. I'm screaming as loud as I can and crying, and my mom tries to stop him but he just hits her out of the way and continues out the door. Seeing my mom being hit only makes me scream and cry louder and I am kicking as hard as I can trying to get away. He walks out the front gate and towards his red Ford pickup truck where some lady is in the passenger seat waiting. I am now having a panic attack at age two and am kicking and swinging my arms as hard as my little body can, trying so hard to get away. That feeling of being held against my will and fighting as hard as I possibly could to get away, only to be held tighter so I couldn't even move is something I still have nightmares about. My screams were deafening, but still I could not scream loud enough to get all the panic out. As he carried me over to the passenger side of his truck and was trying to get me in the door, the neighbor kid came riding up on his bike. I remember looking down and seeing the kids front bike tire about six inches away from the mans cowboy boot and thinking how maybe the bike will run over his foot and it will hurt him so much that he will drop me. That's what I remember the clearest, looking down and hoping that tire would run over his cowboy boot and I would be free.

The kid didn't run over his foot and I was thrown in the truck and comforted by the stranger lady, which only made me cry more. The more I cried, the more he yelled at me to shut up and stop crying. We drove for what seemed forever and I remember not being able to cry anymore. I was still scared out of my mind, and he kept yelling at me, but I could not cry one more drop. I ran out I guess. Next thing I remember, we stopped at some grocery store. I went inside with this guy and the lady and they bought some food and a Styrofoam cup full of worms. I had never seen anything like that and under the circumstances it freaked me out. He yelled at me for that too. On our way out of the store, I remember them buying me a toy from one of those little red machines by the door where you put a quarter in and turn the dial. I don't remember what the toy was but it didn't even matter, it gave me something to squeeze onto and something to take my mind off what was happening.

The next thing I remember we were in the woods setting up camp and there were more people I didn't know. I think there were two other kids and a couple more adults. I watched the guy who took me put up a sheet across some branches in a tree and I could not figure out why he was doing that. When he was done, I asked him. He said it was to hide us while we camped there because we weren't really supposed to be there. Now I may not have even been four years old yet, but I still couldn't believe how stupid that was. Nothing is more natural looking than a white sheet hanging from tree to tree in the forest.

Maybe it was his stupidity or maybe it was something he said, but it was right around then I figured it out that this guy was my dad. I started asking questions about where my mom was and where we were and what was going on and all he kept doing was bad mouthing my mom and telling me how he was going to raise me from now on. I remember that feeling in my gut when he told me that. That sinking feeling you get when you realize you will never see someone again. That only scared me more and made me cry more and his solution to that was to yell at me to stop crying and to threaten me. That continued on until we were sitting around the campfire and he handed me a hot dog he had cooked for me over the fire. It was completely black and crispy and I wouldn't eat it. That made him finally lose it and he hauled off and hit me and told me to eat it. I refused and he kept yelling at me and telling me how I was going to end up a girl if I went back and was raised by my mom, grandma, and aunt and how I was never going to see them again so just shut up and eat. I didn't eat and started being a brat just like all kids do when they don't get what they want. Anytime I was difficult or cried, I got yelled at and hit.

I remember when it was time to go to sleep, I had to sleep in the same sleeping bag as him and he stripped down to his tighty whiteys and that freaked me out. Sleeping in a bag with a stranger in his skivvies wasn't exactly relaxing. I eventually fell asleep though. It had been a big day.

The next day all I remember was going out on a lake in some inflatable raft with him and at least one other kid. I can't remember if there was another one, but I do remember the kid with really curly blond hair. He kept trying to talk to me and I didn't want to talk to him or anyone else. We went out there to go fishing with the Styrofoam cup of worms that were bought earlier and I wanted nothing to do with it.

Then the little curly haired booger eater kept grabbing seaweed or something from the water and putting it in the raft and that grossed me out and gave me a reason to be a bigger brat. I screamed and cried because the seaweed was touching me and it was slimy. That finally set my dad over the edge I guess, because he went off on me telling me how much of a sissy I was, how being raised by women will turn me into one, and how he couldn't put up with me anymore and didn't want me. So he took me back home, dropped me off, and drove away. Never saw him again until I was sixteen.

There's a lot of that I don't remember, like the ride when he took me back home or how he left me, but I can clearly see, like it happened yesterday, being in that raft with the seaweed and the curly haired kid, the tighty whitey stranger getting into my sleeping bag, the burnt hot dog, the white sheet camouflaging us in the woods, and more than anything, I can see myself praying that the bicycle tire would run over his cowboy boot. Those images will be stuck in my head forever. That feeling of not being able to get away, that claustrophobic panic feeling, still to this day stops me in my tracks sometimes. The effects that had on me will never be resolved. I was scared to death of all strangers and was afraid to leave the house for years. Playing in the front yard brought on panic attacks and I was glued to my mom's side as much as I could. I remember when anyone would meet me, they would tell my mom or grandma how shy I was and how well behaved I was because I never said a word. I grew up being afraid of everyone.

For a few years on my birthday, I would get a card from him telling me how much he would like to see me again. I never wanted to and neither did my mom, so after a few years of not hearing back from me, he gave up I guess. I think it would have meant a lot more if maybe he would have tried to contact me more often than just once a year on my birthday when it was convenient, but that never happened. He never paid any child support so legally I didn't have to see him and even though it was tougher on my mom, I think it was better for both of us. I'm sure she talked to him a lot more than I was aware of and I'm sure she tried very hard to keep him from seeing me which was the right thing to do.

I never knew what was going on with them until that one day when I was sixteen and my mom told me my dad was in Reno and wanted to meet with her to discuss all the child support crap and I could go if I wanted to. She told me I didn't have to but it was my decision. I decided I wanted to go. I was a teenager and thought I could handle anything and it wouldn't be that big of a deal. So we went to the McDonald's to meet him. My mom had asked my uncle to conveniently be there as well in case anything happened. When we got there, I was a lot more nervous than I had thought I would be. We walked in and when I first saw him, I got that panicky feeling but just kept quiet. He was sitting in a booth by the window, my mom sat down across from him and I sat behind my mom in the next booth. I don't remember how he greeted us, but I know I didn't say a word. They started out talking but I could tell it wouldn't be long before they started arguing, which is why it's always good to meet in a public place. After they talked for a while, he asked to talk to me. My mom went over to my uncle, and I sat down across from him. He had ordered two cheeseburgers and offered me one and I said no. I don't really remember the conversation, but I know after he muddled his way through some small talk, he started to tell his side of the story. He told me how he wanted full custody of me and that's why he took me and how my mom had been telling me all these lies about him and what had really happened with all of that. That's when I got angry and told him how my mom had told me nothing about it or him, I remember exactly what happened and that's why I don't want anything to do with him. He kept blaming my mom and telling me how she was the bad person in all of this and how I wasn't raised right and it's not his fault. After a few more minutes of listening to this shit, I had enough. I got up and started to walk out and my mom was close behind. When I sat down in the car, I lost it and cried. I don't know why but I couldn't control it. My mom kept asking what he said and why I was crying, but I wouldn't tell her. It didn't matter. She didn't need to hear it and I didn't need to repeat it. I'm sure she was tired of dealing with him and I knew I never wanted to see or talk to him again so it didn't matter. I have never seen or heard from him again.

I get asked if I would ever want to meet him again if I ever had the chance. There is no way I would want to meet him. I mean there is that part of me that would love to go up to him and just beat the shit out of him for everything he did to my mom and me, but realistically, no. I have no desire to know someone like that. Someone that would hit a woman, selfishly kidnap a child, belittle and hit him, not pay child support, and then not even be man enough to admit he was wrong. No way.

I have no idea where he is now. I have no idea if he is even still alive. Don't care.

2

S O EVEN THOUGH I did not grow up to be a woman like my dear old father told me I was going to, I was however primarily raised by women. I lived with my mom and my aunt, and during the day when they worked, my grandma and grandpa took care of me. That was pretty much the extent of my family, besides my uncle Martin who I didn't see very much or really know at all until later on in life. I saw him maybe twice a year on Thanksgiving and Christmas and I was scared of him so I never talked to him. I was scared of everybody, but he was this strange guy that showed up twice a year to eat and he had really long hair and this massive beard, so he was extra scary. He and my grandpa didn't get along very well which is why he didn't come around very often. Martin was a hippie and my grandpa didn't approve of that and after he got in trouble for smoking pot or something, my grandpa wouldn't talk to him for years. From what I hear, they never really did like each other.

I didn't know too much about my aunt either. She was married before I came along and then one Christmas morning, her husband told her to go get some snacks and stuff from the store and when she got back home, he was gone and had left a note saying he didn't want to be married anymore. That was pretty bad and I guess that's a big part of why she became so bitter and negative. That and growing up thinking that showing emotion was wrong, which she passed on to me. She was a nurse and worked different hours all the time so I didn't see her on a regular basis, but when I did, I always felt stupid around her. If I got excited about something I got looked at like I was an idiot and if I had an opinion on something I would get a disgusted, "Oh Jesus Christ" accompanied by an eye roll. It was like she was mad at me for having likes and dislikes and opinions. I started to just keep quiet and keep my thoughts to myself because it started to hurt when I would show some honest emotions and then get mocked or scolded for them. I learned it's a lot less humiliating to just keep it all inside.

I know that it isn't all her fault, she was raised that way and for a long time I blamed her for me being so insecure and unemotional, but I have learned that you can't blame anything on other people. As you get older, you can figure out what is working and what isn't and you can change it if you want to.

I do love my aunt and she has helped both my mom and me tremendously throughout the years and I appreciate everything she has done, but I wish it would have been more emotional help and not just financial. I still hate it though when people roll their eyes.

My grandpa, who I called Turk because he always wore this baby blue zip up sweatshirt that had "All American Turkey" written on it with a picture of a turkey, was a very unemotional man. His mom was a very negative and mean lady from what I have heard so I'm sure that's why he didn't say much or show much emotion. He used to hang out outside of Woolworths when he was younger and that's how he met my grandma since she worked there. He wanted to get married right away but since they were both going into the military, they decided to wait until they came back from the war to get married. He joined the Navy and became some kind of jet mechanic and gained a lot of experience and could have come back home and done that for a living and made big bucks, but instead decided to go be a laborer at the railroad only because that is where his dad used to work. He did that all week and mowed lawns on the weekends and that's how he made a living.

From what I hear he wasn't a very caring or supportive father to my aunt, mom, and uncle either. He basically made fun of them all the time and made them feel like crap and never showed he cared. He never wanted to go on vacation or anything with them and when asked if he wanted to go to Hawaii for example, his response was, "Why? I never left anything there." According to him, that's the only reason to go anywhere, because you left something there. He also had the opportunity to invest in a piece of land on the other side of town with three other guys and told them no because, "No one is ever going to want to go all the way over there." A giant mall was built there later. He had a lot of missed opportunities in life it seemed and I hear he changed a lot when I came along. When I heard how mean he used to be to his kids, I couldn't believe it, because he was nothing but nice to me.

My grandma was one of the greatest people I've ever known. She was a truly good person with a big heart. She was so nice, but if you did something to make her mad, you knew it. Not in a mean way, but in a way that let you know what was right and and what was wrong.

She was born in Green Bay and her mom died shortly after she was born. Her dad raised her and eventually married another lady that turned into an evil stepmother and beat her. She never said anything and a few years later, her dad found out about it and divorced her and they moved to Reno.

When she got older she went shopping for some new clothes and couldn't find anything she liked so she got frustrated and decided to join the Army because they would dress her and she wouldn't have to deal with picking out clothes. And that's what she did. She actually made the decision to join the Army solely on wardrobe convenience.

When she came back from the war, she married my grandpa and became a housewife I guess. She was a great mom and all her kids adored her and she was a great grandma to me as well. I spent a lot of time with her growing up because my mom would drop me off at school in the morning and then Gran, as I called her, picked me up and took me to her house until my mom got off work and came and took me home. A lot of times we would stay there for dinner before we went home. Those were good times. Gran, Turk, my mom and me having a nice family dinner. Those are the simple things you take for granted at the time but wish you could go back and do one more time.

During the summer when I didn't go to school, she used to drive all the way across town to pick me up at my mom's work and take me to her house. She spoiled me rotten. I spent all day there, all summer, and had a great time. She had this park bench on the side of her house that overlooked a flowerbed and we called that area Granny Park. We did a lot of sitting and talking while we were on that bench and it was great. I had no friends to play with, and it didn't matter because I was completely happy just playing in the yard or whatever with her. I miss my grandma.

My mom has not only been a great mom, but she has also been a great friend. Her and I have been through a lot together and I am happy I was an only child raised by a single parent. I realize and appreciate what she has done for me more and more everyday and respect her for being able to do it.

She was the youngest and the most picked on as she was growing up. Like I said, my grandpa wasn't a very caring father and he seemed to pick on her the most. He used to call her names, criticize her, and tell her he wasn't worried about her getting kidnapped because no one would want her anyway and they would have to pay him to give her back. What a guy, huh? So, because of the parent of the year, she naturally grew up with some insecurities. When she moved to Montana and married my dad, he wasn't much nicer. He used to belittle her and hold her down and scare her with snakes, which is why she is deathly afraid of them today. After she had me and she divorced him, he told her she would never be able to raise a kid on her own, I would grow up to be a loser, etc. Same old bullshit from some asshole.

And through all that, she proved him and everyone else wrong about her being able to handle raising me. She sacrificed a lot for me and had to take a lot of crappy jobs to be able to support us but she did it. She not only did it, but she did it well and has always been encouraging of me and has never been mean to me or never has made fun of me or taken out her frustrations on me. She is the only one that has ever been there for me no matter what and has always been supportive. I think she has done a fantastic job of raising me and my opinion is the only one that counts.

Being an only child raised by a single parent, we naturally became close. And when I came back after being kidnapped by my dad, I was so afraid of being taken away from my mom again, that I was glued to her so she really had no choice but to like me!

I remember when she took me to my first day of kindergarten. It was a traumatic day. She takes me into my classroom and meets my teacher and hangs out for a minute or two. I'm completely overwhelmed by all of the kids there, but sit down at my desk anyway. Of course some kid starts talking to me and I was too shy so I think I just ignored him. So as I'm sitting there, I feel scared by all the people but my mom is still there so I think I can manage. I finally start talking to this kid a little bit and then my mom comes over and tells me she is leaving. Oh shit. She leaves with the other parents and this kid keeps talking to me like it's no big deal that our parents aren't there and we are all alone with a bunch of strangers. All the other kids are laughing and playing and I get nervous and start to panic. I look out the window and see my mom headed to her car and I freak out. I start to get that claustrophobic panic feeling and

I go running out the nearest door which leads out to the playground, not the parking lot, so I can't get to her because of the giant chain link fence. I grasp onto that fence and scream as loud as I can like I've been put into prison for something I didn't do. The teacher comes out after me and tries to get me off the fence but having some strange lady pull on me is only making me scream more and hold on tighter. My mom hears me along with the rest of the city, and comes back and tries to get me to let go, but my little fingers are locked into that fence so tight a tractor couldn't pull me off. I can remember how much my fingers hurt and how loud my screams were. It was intense. I was drawing quite the crowd by now and I think my mom was too embarrassed to be mad at me. I don't remember how but eventually they got me to let go and go back in the classroom. I think my mom stayed a while longer but she did eventually leave and I did stay the rest of the day in the classroom. It was quite the first impression I made which probably explains why I didn't have any friends in school.

After that monstrosity, the next couple of school years went by pretty uneventful. It took a while for me to make friends since they all thought if they even said hi to me I would go running towards the street screaming and crying, but eventually I had a few kids I could at least talk to. I don't have many memories from my elementary schools years. I got made fun of for stupid stuff, but so did everyone else. I got made fun of a lot more after I got my glasses that made my eyes the size of dinner plates, but still, that was nothing.

So school was becoming easier mainly because it was becoming more familiar, but I was still way too shy to have any fun and all I ever looked forward to was going home and playing with my toys by myself. It was getting better, but still anytime I went anywhere with my mom or Gran, I would be nervous and it always felt like I had to keep myself from running away. I didn't like being around strangers and I still don't today. I used to hate to go get new shoes because in those days, they had someone there that measured your feet, got your shoes, and then put them on for you, and that was way too much time with a stranger for me. Same with getting a haircut. I dreaded going and sitting there that close to someone and having to answer stupid questions like, "What's your favorite color?" when all I wanted to do was be quiet. Then they would ask how I liked my shoes or my haircut and I would always just say, "Fine" because I didn't care, I just wanted to leave.

I used to hate going to the dentist too. I think it was my first time going to the dentist that ruined it for me. I remember how nervous I was because I had no clue what going to the dentist was all about. I sat in the waiting room and of course all I could hear was high pitched drills and every kid that came out looked scared and had gauze in their mouth. Finally it was my turn and some lady brought me to the back and sat me in this bright yellow chair that leaned way back. There were about five or so chairs back there and a couple of them had kids in them. A man with a mustache was leaning over one of the kids with his fingers in the kids mouth and another lady was watching. The lady that brought me back was very nice and I think she brushed my teeth or something for me. As I was sitting there I could hear the man yelling at the kid to stop it. I couldn't look over to see what was going on, but of course it freaked me out. The lady told me to just relax so I tried.

After she got done cleaning my teeth, she took me to get x-rays. I went to another room and sat in another yellow chair and she put the fifty pound blanket over me and took pictures of my teeth. Again I heard the man yelling at the kid, "Stop whining, I'm not going to tell you again." I started getting really nervous now, but the lady told me to relax and go back to the first chair I sat in and the dentist would be right there to see me. As I sat down, the one kid was done and was crying. He walked by and just kept crying as he left. The dentist man then went over to the other kid and started sticking his fingers in his mouth. I guess the kid was moving around too much because he kept getting yelled at to sit still. I started to get that good old panicked feeling I was used to and wanted to run. After the dentist was done with that kid he followed him out to talk to his parents or something and the lady that cleaned my teeth wasn't around, so I was all alone in there. I started thinking about how much he yelled at the other kids and how scared both those kids looked when they left. I didn't want to get yelled at, the last man that yelled at me beat me and made me have panic attacks.

There was nobody to stop me if I wanted to run. All I had to do was make it to the waiting room and tell Gran and my mom I was too scared to go through with it. The dentist came back in and went to the back to wash his hands or something. As he walked by me, he smiled at me and told me he would be right back. Maybe it was the way he chewed his gum or maybe it was his mustache, but I wanted no part of him and I had to get out of there. I jumped off the chair and ran towards the door.

I made it to the receptionist desk, all I had to do was open the door that lead out to the waiting room. I reached out and grabbed the doorknob, turned it and pulled it open as fast as I could. So fast that I couldn't get out of the way of the door in time and whacked myself in the head with it. Damn near knocked myself out. That slowed me down enough for people to catch me and the last thing I remember is seeing people trying to hold back their laughter. I don't know if I went back in or not. I really hit my head good. I admit, it must have looked pretty funny though.

I continued going to that dentist for a few more years and every time I went, he was yelling at kids to shut up or sit still. I never said a word and I always sat still when he was working on me because I didn't want to get yelled at. Although a couple of times when something hurt and I flinched, he would poke me on the chest really hard and would yell at me to quit moving. He did that to everybody so I just went with it. He was mean though. Even when he wasn't yelling at us kids, he was still pretty rough and rude to us. But when he went out to talk to the parents afterward, he was the nicest guy in the world. That's why no one believed me when I told them why I tried to run away from him the first time. They thought I was just scared of the dentist and since I was afraid of everybody that it was just me being a baby. A few years after I stopped going to him, it came out that he was abusing children so he lost his license and went to jail and everything. Told you so.

Being an only child had it's advantages and disadvantages. It was nice not only being the only child, but also being the only child in the entire family. No cousins or anyone taking away from my Christmas presents! I was it, so I got spoiled. I had a million toys all to myself, so that was a big advantage. The biggest advantage though was the relationship with my mom. It wouldn't have been so close if I would have had a brother or sister. I think with both friends and family, it's better to have a few really close ones rather than a bunch of acquaintances that you call friends and a bunch of third cousins twice removed that you call family.

One disadvantage was since I was the only child in the family there were no other children to compare me to, so as a child I was expected to know more and act older, but as I got older, I was still treated like a child. I didn't have an older brother or anyone for them to see how much kids change from year to year, so it was kind of frustrating to be told I have no common sense at age seven but then was still expected to think girls had cooties when I was seventeen. My mom was the only one that wasn't like that with me though, she let me do my own thing and for the most part, let me make my own decisions and accepted me for being an idiot kid and understood it.

The only other disadvantage of being the only child was it left me with a lot of alone time. It was fine, but as I got older, I got really used to being alone and not having to talk all the time, so it came across as I was stuck up or didn't like the people I was around. That wasn't the case at all, I was just used to being quiet and was used to having so many hours a day to myself. I'm still like that now. It comes across as if I'm moody or whatever but I spent so much time alone growing up, that I got used to not talking and sometimes now days, I just don't feel like talking. It's not much more complicated than that. I'm just a quiet guy.

A lot of my alone time was spent playing with toys, but somehow I started to draw. I don't remember what got me into it, probably just doodling, but I used to draw everything I saw. I started out mainly just copying cartoons, but it got me going. I'm sure Gran and everybody was just being nice when they told me how good my drawings were, but it felt so good to be complimented on them that it made me want to keep doing it. I think that's how everybody figures out what they like to do or not. If people are encouraging and complimentary towards what you are doing or making, you automatically want to do it more. How else do you know what you like to do when you're little? You like everything because it's all new and exciting and the only way you know if you're good at something is because someone else tells you you are. That's why you like doing it, because you are good at it, and how do you know you are good at it? People tell you! It's not fair, other people tell you what to like and dislike right off the bat before you know any better, and by the time you figure out what you really like to do deep down and truthfully, it's too late.

People started telling me I liked to draw in elementary school and I think that was the only way I made friends. I remember the first time I got noticed for my drawing. I don't remember what grade I was in but it was pretty early on like third or fourth grade. We all had to draw and color a full bodied picture of a member of the faculty at the school and they would be put up in the main hallway.

All the names of the teachers, teachers assistants, lunch room people, etc., were put into a hat. I randomly selected the janitor. That was good because he had a certain characteristic look. Black dyed hair that was receding, mustache, five o' clock shadow all the time, skinny, always wore a uniform, and always had a cigarette hanging out of his mouth. After we drew the names from the hat, they gave us a little picture of our person to go off of and we were supposed to draw just their face first on a separate piece of paper. Don't know why we had to do that but I did what I was told. The way I looked at it, we were supposed to draw their face so it looked like them so I got into it. I put in wrinkles, made shadows, and even started dotting in his five o' clock shadow, when the teacher came along and looked at it she told me it looked really good, but I was spending too much time on it and I should just start drawing the real one now because everyone else is almost done.

So I started in on that one and got into it again. As I was finishing up coloring the janitor, the other kids started coming over and looking at it and they were getting excited asking me how I did that. I didn't think it was that good because I felt rushed, but everyone else seemed to like it and said it looked just like the janitor, so I was happy. When the teacher came around and looked at it she went on and on about how good it was, so my popularity was really starting to skyrocket now.

A couple of days later they hung up all of our drawings in the hallway and we got to go look at them. After looking at the drawings of teachers that apparently all have circles for heads, I saw mine but something was missing from it. The cigarette I had drawn hanging out of his mouth was gone. The teacher told me how they had to cut it off because they didn't want to glorify smoking. I was mad because I worked hard at coloring that cigarette just right so it looked like it was burning, and now they cut it off but left a little quarter inch or so part of it where it came out of his mouth so it looked like he had this little white drool coming out of his mouth. Let that be a lesson, don't trust your art with anyone.

I continued drawing all throughout school and that seemed to be the only way I got attention. Anytime I would draw something, the other kids would watch and the teacher always liked it, so I kept doing it. I even won a contest one year for drawing a bald eagle for an air pollution poster. That was my big moment. It's all been pretty much downhill since that.

3

MY MOM WAS able to move out of my aunt's house, so we moved into a duplex on Merchant Ct. which wasn't too far away. Once again, I had my own room, another advantage of being an only child. It was nice, we had our own garage, our own backyard, and it was like starting over. My mom even started dating again. She started dating this guy with a mustache, who I will just call Larry, and he was all right I guess. It obviously took a while for me to warm up to him, but he was never mean to me or anything so I had no problem with him.

Don't have many memories about him because I don't think I talked to him that much and I pretty much just avoided him. I wanted to stay out of the way as much as possible. It was just better that way for everyone. I didn't realize it at the time, but that must have been really tough for my mom to try and date with a smelly little brat like me running around. He was cool though. He put up with me. He played with me once in a while and even taught me a few things. Like this one time he was watching television over at our house and smoking. He finished the cigarette and then pulled out some little rectangular papers and was putting this green stuff in them. I asked him what he was doing and he told me he was just rolling some new cigarettes. I was fascinated by this and as he rolled up a few more, he taught me how to do it and asked me if I wanted to try rolling one. I did and had no clue until I was much older and my mom told me that those weren't cigarettes. Another thing I can put on my resume, a five year old doobie roller. It wasn't a big deal though, I didn't know any better and after all, it was the eighties.

It's not like I ended up being addicted to pot or anything. I never even really smoked it. Of course I tried it when I was in high school, but who didn't? I never really got into it though, all it did was make me tired, so I didn't see what all the hoopla was about. There are so many people who live for it and I just don't get it. Maybe because I don't have an addictive personality. I don't care if people smoke it though, I'm not one of those people who gets all pissy and goes out of my way to ruin it for everyone else just because I don't like it and feel left out. What people do is their business and if it doesn't effect your life, then stay out of it.

Anyway, if that's all I remember about Larry, then that's a good thing. They eventually broke up and my doobie rolling career was over.

When I was seven years old or so, we moved into our first home on Randolph Drive across town. It was a very nice blue, two story house and I not only had my own room, but also my own bathroom. I had really hit the big time now. But now that we had moved, I was zoned to go to a different school. I didn't really want to go to a new school and start all over again and after my mom talked with me and Gran about it, they decided to let me stay at the same school I had been going to. Given my track record of keeping my cool on first days of school and my inability to make friends easily, it was decided to not mess with a good thing and keep me going to school across town where I knew the kids and where it would be better for my psyche. It was a longer drive for them to take me and pick me up, but in the long run, it was easier. We just kept using my aunts address so it was no big deal.

After our German Shepard Chauncy went to doggy heaven, we got a German Shepard mix and soon after that, we got a Golden Retriever. The German Shepard's name was Bandit and the Retriever's name was Bucky and they were my main friends for most of my childhood. I used to play with them for hours and even though Bandit was very protective and would bark and want to attack most people, he let me tackle him and chase him and never did anything to me. Bucky was a typical Retriever that was always hyper and only wanted to play ball. Many years later he chased a ball into a cactus and got a needle in his eye and had to have his eye removed. I always felt bad about that because I was the one that threw the ball. I didn't do it on purpose but still, poor guy.

My mom was really starting to do well, she had a good job and was able to get this house with a little help from Gran and my aunt, and she started dating another guy with a mustache. I will just call him Russ. Russ was a landscaper or something like that and seemed to be an all right guy. I was slowly starting to get over my fear of strangers and right away he was cool to me. He would always want to take me wherever he was taking my mom and he would always play with me and be interested in what I was doing. It was weird to have a guy around that was so nice to me. It got to the point where I almost looked forward to him coming over. I think he was even the one who put up a basketball hoop above our garage for me. He taught me a little about sports and he and my mom were getting along really well, so everything was going along good.

I still didn't have any friends to play with, but I didn't need any, I had the dogs, a basketball hoop and my own bathroom. And I got a new bike for Christmas, so I was set. I spent a lot of time out in the front yard pretending I was playing basketball with someone else. I became the best one on none basketball player in the neighborhood, if not the country. I didn't even think of how stupid I must have looked out there shooting the ball with one hand and blocking it with the other.

I also was a pretty mean one man football team. I would start out snapping the ball to myself, dropping back and throwing it across the yard but still high enough so I could go run underneath it and catch it, then break a few tackles before getting tackled just short of the goal line. I would then line up, snap the ball to myself, turn and hand the ball to myself and dive over nothing to score the touchdown. That must have looked pretty stupid as well. I'm sure the neighbors loved me. I developed quite the imagination though. Those basketball and football games were very detail oriented and intense. I wasn't just running around like an idiot, I knew exactly what I was doing, and in my mind, I saw the other players trying to tackle me. It never even crossed my mind that people might be watching me. I wish I could go back and not care like that again. Just be in my own little world and do whatever popped into my head without an ounce of self consciousness. Why do we have to lose that freedom? Only kids, animals and crazy people have that true freedom.

When I wasn't voluntarily beating myself up and scaring the neighbors with my athletic abilities, I was playing with my little G.I. Joe action figures. I called that "playing men". Sounds kind of weird now, but back then it just meant playing with toys. The backyard was a great place to play men. Russ had helped landscape the yard so there were a lot of rocks and plants, so it was a great place to play war with the men. I would spend hours out there and if I had to come inside, I would line all of them up on the carpet and make them play football. That's all I needed to keep myself entertained, action figures, a basketball and football, and some paper to draw on. I didn't need any friends.

I used to ride my bike a lot too, just not very far away from home. I had a Schwinn bike that I named Bert because it was black and yellow like from Bert and Ernie. I was weird. I also had an imaginary friend named Maynard. He later passed away after suffocating in my aunts suitcase on her way to Hawaii. Better than drowning in a milkshake though. Like I said, I was weird.

Anyway, it was a nice bike. I had gotten one of those mini license plates with my name on it when we went to Disneyland, so I put it on the back of my bike underneath the seat, and that added a touch of class. One day I had just gotten back from a spin around the block and parked my bike on the sidewalk and started to shoot around with the basketball. Then this kid is walking by and stops and looks at me and then looks at my sweet license plate and asks me, "Is your name Travis?" I looked at him and said, "Duh!" If I was him, I would have kept walking if some kid was a smart ass like that and said that to me, but instead he invited me to his show that he was putting on in his garage with his sister. He lived around the block and admission was a dollar, so I could go if I wanted to. I tried to play it cool and act like I wasn't excited that someone was talking to me and had invited me to do something, so I think I just told him I might go. He walked away and I continued to bounce the basketball until he was out of sight, then I ran inside and asked my mom for a dollar and asked her if I could go. She gave me a dollar and before I knew it, it was showtime.

I was one of maybe four people that showed up to the show so I got a front row seat. I remember his garage being very dark but also very well decorated with streamers and neon colored things. It was very nice looking and I was excited. I sat there and looked around at who else was in the crowd and I think there were a couple of construction workers and another kid or two. I sat in my seat and patiently waited for the show to start. All of a sudden Van Halen started blasting and the kid came out all decked out in rocker gear with his sister and started dancing and jumping around. It was quite the show. They had quite the stage presence and it really was a shame more people weren't there to witness it. I don't know if this was a one time event or if it was an ongoing show, but Van Halen never sounded so good. Before I knew it, the show was over and I don't remember exactly what happened, but I think I just went back home and told my mom how cool it was. It wasn't so much that the show itself was cool, it was that I got invited to go and that made me feel cool.

The kids name was Arnold, and since he lived only one street over, we started hanging out together. I of course went to a different school than he did, but we hung out after school and on the weekends sometimes. He only wanted to hang out with me because of my wide variety of toys, but I didn't care because I finally had a friend. He started coming over all the time and I had someone to play basketball and football with. That must have been a big relief for the neighbors to see me actually playing basketball against another person. I was however, not nearly as good playing against him as I was playing against myself. It was a lot tougher and not as much fun because I kept losing. We also started playing one on one football games and fortunately for me, he was just as stupid as I was, so now there were two kids out there throwing the ball to themselves and running around. Unfortunately for the neighbors, we started using their yards as our field. Mailboxes were the end zones and the sidewalk was out of bounds, so we just helped ourselves to every ones yard in between. Now days, if some little pecker-necks were playing in my yard, I would yell at them to stay out of my yard, but back then no one really ever said anything to us. It was a lot more fun playing football against someone else.

I also introduced him to playing men. That really ended up being what we did most of the time. I remember him coming over and asking me what I wanted to do. I almost always suggested, "Play men?" and he almost always agreed. So we would play men for hours either in my room or in the backyard. I think he eventually started liking me, not just my toys, and I started to like him, not just because he was the only kid that talked to me. I think it helped that we went to different schools too. If we went to the same one, I'm sure we wouldn't have been as good of friends back then. He was one of the popular kids at his school and I was this nerd with giant coke bottle glasses at mine, so I'm sure we wouldn't have hung out together at the same school. It was also good we went to different ones, because it gave us something to talk about and look forward to. At least for me, I looked forward to going home after school and playing men or football with someone I actually liked, not just someone I had to be around all day at school. And it was always fun to hear what was going on at the school I was supposed to go to and hear all about those kids. It was just nice to have a real friend.

As our athletic abilities and interests grew, we started a little game called Spitball. We would chew gum or candy or whatever, take our baseball bats, spit and swing and try to connect. It was disgusting but it entertained us for years. Sometimes we would even eat cookies first and then spit because it made our spit thicker and it would make a louder splatting noise when we hit it. It was gross, but it's something I still think about and it was a good memory.

Another good memory is when Turk would take Arnold and me to the UNR football games. I looked forward to it every week we got to go. The neighbors across the street from Gran and Turk's house worked at the university and could get us tickets whenever we wanted to go, so my mom would drive Arnold and me up to their house and drop us off where we would pile in the old white Maverick car and head to the game. My mom and Gran would hang out all day so it really worked out for everyone. When we got to the game, we would find Turk's neighbors and tailgate with them. Arnold and I would play one on one football while all of them drank and ate. It was always good food and a lot of it. When it was game time, we would go get our seats and sit with all the old drunk guys. There weren't many kids in that section, but it wouldn't have been as much fun if there were. It was great the way it was.

After the game we would go back to Gran and Turk's and Arnold and I would go play more football in their front yard. We would usually try to recreate the game we just saw. We couldn't get enough football. Then my mom would load us up in her car and take us home. Those were good times. Again, it's that simple kind of stuff I miss the most.

Russ and my mom were doing good and he eventually moved in with us, which I thought was good. He was always really nice to me and he always took me to do fun stuff. It was really nice to have a man always around to kind of teach me stuff, like sports, mowing the lawn, and lifting weights and such. My mom did a great job teaching me stuff, but he knew more about sports. I started to really get comfortable around him and almost looked at him as a "kinda" parent. Since he seemed to be so good with kids, Arnold's mom started using him as her babysitter to watch him and his sister sometimes and he did a good job, so he was a hit with everyone. As far as I knew, even Gran and Turk liked him because he treated my mom and me so well, and did all the manly things my mom needed done around the house. I don't remember what he did for a living, but it was something like landscaping, so everyone thought that was cool. We were a happy little home as far as I knew and all was going well. I started to trust him and and that wasn't easy for me to do since I didn't trust anyone except for my mom and Gran. I especially never trusted or even really liked men with the exception of Turk. But Russ was so nice to me and always wanted to hang out with me, that I eventually let my guard down and liked him. That was a huge mistake.

The three of us used to go to the lake on the weekends and when we got back home, my mom would usually go take a nap and I would go play and Russ would always hang around me. He always wanted to hang out with me when I was in my room and it never was a big deal until I finally let my guard down and started to be comfortable around him. That's when he got me. He always wanted to teach me about sex and told me that it was all guy stuff so I couldn't tell my mom or I would get in big trouble. I didn't really know what the hell was going on but I knew I was uncomfortable and the more I kept pushing him away, the more he tried. He kept telling me I had to learn and I would get in trouble if I didn't behave. I'm not going to get into any details but he never gave up and although it only happened a few times, it messed with my head more than you can imagine. I felt completely stuck. I knew what he was doing was wrong, but I also didn't want to get into trouble and of course I figured he would beat me or make my life worse if I told. I was only eight or nine maybe, so I didn't know any better, so I just kept my mouth shut. I never said anything to anybody, not even Arnold. I basically just made myself believe that it wasn't happening and figured it was just me who thought it was wrong and I didn't want to complain to anyone and act like a baby. I went back to not liking him or trusting him, but pretended as best as I could that I still did so it wouldn't cause a stir. Over time, for whatever reason I'm not sure of, they broke up and he moved out. I still didn't say anything. I was glad he left because I could never really relax after all of that. They still tried to make it work after he had his own place, but it never did.

It was years before I saw him again. He had come over to say hi to my mom I guess. I was in my early teens I think, and was in my room when I heard my mom talking to someone downstairs. I went out and looked over the side and saw him down there. He said hi and commented on how grown up I was. I said hi and just kind of stared at him. After awkwardly being friendly, I went back to my room. They talked for a while and then that was it. Never saw him again. Even after he left, I never said anything.

A few years after that came the breaking news. Literally. He had been arrested for making child porn and it was on the news. Everyone was shocked, even me because all of these years, I didn't know if it was just me or not. No one could have even imagined he was capable of being such a sick fuck. He got busted with tapes of a couple of seven year old girls or something and after word got out on the news, I got asked by my family and everyone if he ever did anything to me. I still didn't say anything. This time I wish I would have. It was a pretty convenient time, but it's not something I could just easily blurt out and say. It's kind of a deep subject that is going to take a while to talk about and it's going to upset my mom and family. That is the number one reason I have never said anything to anybody. I never wanted my mom to get upset about it and blame herself. She's the type of person that will think it was all her fault and will never be able to be convinced otherwise. I would never want to hurt her and none of this was in any way, shape or form, her fault. She had no idea about it because first off, why would that thought even cross her mind that he was like that? People usually don't go around thinking everyone they meet is a child molester until they are proven otherwise, and that sicko was a professional manipulator of parents and children. She never knew because he knew exactly what he was doing and probably had it all planned out since the first day he met us. It was nobody's fault but his. Whatever happened to him to make him be that way is horrible and I wish it didn't happen to him, but it did, so get over it. Have the self respect to end it with yourself and not keep bringing down innocent families with you. He was a sick fuck and I hope he paid for it, but I know he never truly will. I'm not concerned how it affected me anymore, I'm fine now, it's the who knows how many other kids lives he's ruined just so he could selfishly feel better about his. People like him are the ones that should rot in solitary confinement for the rest of their lives. Make them spend the rest of their lives in a cell alone with nothing but their own sick minds. I can never get out of my mind because of him, so why should he? Get the pot smokers out of prison and keep the pedophiles locked up and away from the humans. They serve absolutely no purpose in this world. If I ever do see him again, I will not hesitate to beat him unrecognizable and I will not feel one ounce of guilt afterward. He forever changed me and made me different. He is nothing but a waste of human life.

Moving on . . .

4

SINCE I JUST could not get enough football, I started playing Pop Warner in 1986. I had no idea what to expect or what it was about, but I wanted to sign up anyway. After I signed up they told me they would be calling us in a few days or so to let us know what team I would be on and where to go and all that kind of stuff.

I can remember exactly what it was like when they called. I was at Gran and Turk's watching television and the phone rang. I thought nothing of it and didn't even pay attention when Gran answered it. As she hung up, she made a big announcement to Turk and me that I would be playing for the Reno Bears and Turk looked at me and said, "Well that sounds like a good team!" I was excited but nervous. I didn't really know that much about football or what it was going to be like, but I loved playing in my yard and loved watching it.

I was told to go to Pickett Park and to show up with all my gear. I was dropped off and I was so nervous I almost peed myself. I was this little skinny nerd with giant glasses that now had a strap attached to them so I wouldn't lose them in the violent world of pee wee football, and all the kids just kind of stared at me. I don't remember what we exactly did during that first practice but I do remember the end of it. We had to run from one end of the park to the other three times and that just about killed me. Looking back now, it only ended up to be maybe a half of a mile total, but I had never ran that far before and especially not in a helmet and pads. Towards the end of the run, I started cramping up and getting a side ache and I really thought I was going to die. I had never had any of those things happen before so I might have been more scared than physically tired, but it was still pretty hard. It also didn't help that the whole time we were running, the coaches were screaming at us to run faster and to push it harder. By this point of my life, I was really tired of being screamed at by men, but I just kept going. I eventually finished and was cramping up so bad I could hardly walk. I was so out of breath I thought I was going to pass out and so thirsty there wasn't going to be enough water in the world it seemed.

Practice was over and I saw my mom waiting for me at one end of the park. I tried to walk over to her, but between my legs cramping and my lungs bleeding, it was a lot longer of a walk than it should have been. When I finally got to her, I think I cried. I might have just been crying happy tears because I had survived but I didn't think I wanted to do this anymore. My mom sat down with me at the tables there in the park and she told me it was entirely up to me. I didn't have to do this if I truly didn't want to, nobody was making me do it. If I wanted to quit, fine. If I wanted to keep going, fine. She was and is, a great mom. She let me make my decision and for some reason I decided to keep going back.

The next few practices were better and I eventually got used to running without crying. The coaches put me in at defensive end and told me to just get by the blocker and tackle the guy with the ball. So I did. That was the best coaching advice I've ever had. I remember I just kept getting by the blocker over and over again and then the coach came running up to me and grabbed my face mask and I thought I was in trouble. He was all fired up and looked at me and yelled, "You're doing a damn good job Travis, damn good job!" I will always remember that because it felt so great, especially after how terrible I did with the running and how I almost quit. I was so glad I didn't. I was having so much fun and I really ended up looking forward to going to practice and even running.

The only weird part was everyone on the team went to the same Reno school, where I was zoned to go, but I was the only kid on the team that went to a Sparks school. Arnold started playing too, but he ended up on a different team, so I didn't really know anyone very well on my own team. Regardless, I made it through the season and we were a pretty good team. I don't remember what our record was that year, but I learned a lot and it was exactly what I needed.

At the end of the season we had an awards ceremony at a pizza place. All of the players we expected to win certain awards did, and I really wasn't expecting to get anything except the standard team photo, but somehow the Most Improved Player of the Year went to me. I was shocked and I got to go up and get my jersey number 44 to keep as the award. It made Gran and my mom so proud! That made me want to keep playing more than anything.

The next season I played for the Reno Steelers and it was cool because our uniforms were better and looked just like the pros. We even had the Steeler sticker on one side of our helmet. The coaches were a lot nicer to. The head coach, who I will just call Coach, was a really nice guy with a mustache who didn't believe that you had to yell at the players to motivate them and I liked that. Who ever it was that started that stereotype of coaches being drill instructors, really ruined it for a lot of kids. It's a game. It is not life or death. Motivation through fear is not the only option. I will always respect and work harder for someone who respects me enough to treat me like a human and not build his or her own ego up by knocking me down. I'm there to have fun and learn, not to be talked down to and not to learn how to spend the rest of my life trying to live up to the fictitious perfection they will have me believe.

I do understand why it can be good to be a hard ass at times though. And the main point of that is *at times.* Some people need to be yelled at, some need to be talked to. If you do either all the time, it will lose it's effect, so do only what is needed and know that everyone is an individual. Treat them that way and respect that.

Anyway, Coach was a good guy and a good coach. I played defensive end again and we ended up winning our division or whatever they called it. Because we won, we got to go to California and play for a regional championship. That was big. I don't remember where in California, but we all had to pile on a Greyhound bus and get hotel rooms. It was all very exciting. Unfortunately, no one picked me to room with them and I got stuck having Coach and one of the other coaches as my roommates. I had to sleep in the same bed as Coach, which was weird, but he didn't get down to his tighty whiteys or anything like some people in my past. The next day when he talked to my mom and Gran, he just told them how he should make me be the kicker because all I do is kick in my sleep.

It was weird to be traveling somewhere to play football, we felt like pros. Usually all we had to do was have our parents drop us off across town and play a game and then go home, but now we had people feeding us and got to stay in a fancy hotel room and had a curfew. When we finally got to play the game, it wasn't as exciting anymore. California grows their kids a lot bigger and faster than us and we lost. We loaded back up on the bus and headed back home a little more tired and a lot more humble. It was a good season though, one of my favorites of all time. Coach and Gran got along great and they kind of became like friends. It was sad to see the season end and to know that I was going to have a new coach the following year.

1988 was the year of the Reno Raiders and contact lenses. They really did have something to do with each other, because it was the first year I remember playing football without my glasses and it made it a lot easier. I'm pretty much blind without my glasses so wearing them limited my peripheral vision so much, I couldn't see the ball coming at me until it was right in front of me. Once I got contacts, I was catching everything and I moved from defensive end to tight end and even had a play designed for me. I still remember what the play was called; rip bone 24 power pass. That just meant I was going to run straight down the field and they would throw it to me. The first time they called it in a game, I scored a touchdown and it was great. Gran and my mom were proud. I caught a few more that season and we ended up being a pretty good team. I think we went undefeated but we didn't get to go to California or anything. I became a huge Oakland/Los Angeles Raiders fan that year because I loved wearing the black and silver uniforms and Bo Jackson was my favorite player. I started learning all about the history of the Raiders and have been a fan ever since, even through the tough times.

I think it was also that year that Arnold and I went to California to go to football camp. It was somewhere in Northern California and we spent a week there with hundreds of other kids. Our moms drove us down there and we had our own room and it was kind of like being in college. Actually it was probably held at a college campus, but I can't remember which one.

We had a dorm room and we would eat at the cafeteria and practice football all day. The camp was run by all kinds of different pro players and coaches and that was the biggest highlight of my life at the time. Our first day we all had to sit in the bleachers and listen to them tell us what we were going to be going through for the next week. Matt Millen was one of the speakers that stood out to me because he was so mean. Intimidating us was his role I guess. He did a good job of it though, because everyone did what he said.

After the orientation, we found out what groups we would be in and who we would be practicing with. Since there were hundreds of kids of all ages we had to break up into age groups just like Pop Warner, so Arnold and I were on different teams again. For some reason I got put into a group that seemed to have a lot of older kids in it and they were huge. I got run over all over the place by these guys and the coaches put me in at different positions, so not only did I get pushed around by the other players, I got pushed around and yelled at by the coaches because I had no idea what I was doing. It got better after a few practices and I started getting the hang of it and I could keep up at least.

The playing wasn't as much fun as the learning from pro players. Jerry Rice, Tom Rathman, Matt Millen and a whole bunch of others were there to teach us. Jerry Rice told us about the Super Bowl he was in and how to become a better receiver, Rathman taught us how to hold onto the ball better and run people over and the most memorable part for me was Ronnie Lott taught us how to defend passes and how to tackle better. He was and still is one of my favorite players and I was star struck when I saw him. He was teaching a small group of us and when he came up to me after one of our drills and told me how to defend a pass better, I just about shit myself. That was a great day.

On our last day there, we had a game day where our parents could watch. I didn't get too much playing time because I was way out of my league, those guys were big and fast and it's for the best I didn't play much, I would have just embarrassed myself. It was a great week though, one of my favorite times and it was great to meet real pro players and coaches. It really made me love the game more and I really wanted to keep getting better at it. The best part though was meeting Ronnie Lott and having him teach me something. That made the whole week for me.

I finished my Pop Warner career on the Reno Mustangs in 1989. That was a weird year because we only had about fifteen people total on the team. It wasn't so much a team as it was a small gathering of kids wearing the same uniforms. Just about everyone played both on offense and defensive and since no one was really used to doing that, we weren't very good. I played tight end and linebacker. I really liked playing linebacker, it was the most fun position I had played yet. Getting a running start and hitting someone was a lot better than catching a touchdown and I was really starting to love playing this game. Even though we only won half of our games that season, it was still fun and I learned a lot.

Playing sports as a kid is important I think. Not important like war or life threatening diseases or anything, but important in a way I didn't realize until later on in life. I can always tell if a person played sports when they were younger because they seem to let things go easier than people who haven't played. If something goes wrong or unplanned, they can adapt much easier and not let it ruin their whole day. My theory is they have learned from playing sports that you are going to make mistakes and fail from time to time. When I played football, I missed dozens of tackles, dropped hundreds of easy catches, and lost many games, all in front of a crowd. I learned to have a short memory and to just acknowledge I screwed up, try to not let it happen again and move on. Things don't always go according to plan, actually they rarely ever do, so you have to expect that and be ready to adapt and not obsess over something you may not be able to change anyway. I have worked with people who have had something go wrong and the whole day is shot because of it. It has turned into a horrible day for them and they spend the next three days thinking about it and worrying about it. Sports will teach you that mistakes and the unexpected *will* happen, so let it go and move on and try to do better next time. Perfection doesn't exist. It's best to learn that early on in life.

There are people who think sports is stupid and too much importance is placed on it and winning, which sometimes is true. There are plenty of gym teachers and coaches out there that are in denial about being failed athletes and are taking it out on their students and players and that is stupid, I agree, but you shouldn't base your judgment on some dickhead coach trying to live his life through yours and completely turn your back to all the other positives you will get out of it. Look at the big picture and see other opportunities, not just the one dickhead that yelled at you and told you that you weren't good enough. There are dickheads everywhere, if you let them get to you and make your decisions for you, you will never have control over your life. Don't let people tell you what to think. Mainly it is the media that is the one telling us what to think. They have turned sports into the single most important thing in the entire world. There is more coverage of a football game than there is of the war. A football player is out of next weeks game with a pulled hamstring and we have to hear about it for a week, but a soldier dies in Iraq and all they do is show his picture and his rank for a few seconds and that's it.

And as much as I love sports, I cannot stand these sports writers and analysts that have now become mini celebrities by talking about something they know nothing about on TV and the radio. I don't find them very insightful and I don't need to be told what my opinion is. I can watch a game and form my own opinion without having to listen to some jackass over complicate it by dumbing it down for me. They have the easiest job in the world, all they have to do is follow a player or team and be opinionated, criticize, and try to predict. Those are the absolute easiest things in the world for a human to do. And most of the time they can't even do that right because even they know how easy and pointless their job is so they stray away from their honest opinion and say something just for shock value. All of them are just grown men who failed at sports and have never outgrown high school gossip. You have to question people who follow other people for a living.

Kind of got off track there. Anyway, I think sports is good for kids. It teaches them to be tougher, both physically and mentally and it gives them more confidence to try and succeed, realizing to not give up right away if it doesn't go according to plan.

It's also good for adults. It gives us something to get into and feel like we are a part of without any repercussions. I don't understand how some people think watching a game and getting into it or following a certain team is so stupid and such a waste of time, yet they get all hopped up and involved in watching a movie or talking about a television series or reading a book. It's all just entertainment. We all need our escapes to be able to cope with the prison of our realities and that's all sports is–it's an escape.

5

IN THE WINTER of 1990 Gran passed away. The night before, we had one of the biggest snow storms ever in Reno and it dumped a couple of feet of snow. My mom woke me up the next morning like she always did so I could get ready for school. She would always wake me up before she left for work and Gran would come over and take me to school. Because of the snow, school was canceled that day, but we weren't sure if Gran knew or not. As my mom was getting ready to go to work, the phone rang and I answered it. It sounded like Turk, but he said it was Martin, which is my uncles name. He sounded flustered and then said to have my mom call him back. I hung up and told my mom to call Martin back because that's what it sounded like to me. She called Martin but he said he didn't call, so she probably just figured it was a wrong number or something.

My mom went out to warm up her car in the garage and as she was out there in her car the phone rang again and again I answered. It was Turk and I knew it was him this time. He wanted me to get my mom, so I ran out to the garage and told her to come back in. She came back, picked up the phone and then started crying. I had no idea what was going on, but my mom was balling her eyes out and then she told me. I didn't really understand death, I had never known anybody that died, but seeing my mom that upset made me understand a little better. I think she kind of explained it to me and once I figured out that I was never going to see my grandma again, I couldn't cry enough and was in shock. My uncle came over a little later to take my mom and me up to Gran and Turks house because he had a truck that could make it in the snow and my mom couldn't have driven in her condition. I wasn't afraid of him anymore but it was weird to see him all teary eyed. That was one of the longest drives I have ever been on. It was a white out and we could only go about fifteen miles an hour and my mom was a wreck and Martin was trying to keep it together and drive. When we finally got there, my aunt and her boyfriend were already there with Turk and I remember walking in and it was the first time I had ever seen Turk cry or show any emotion really. He looked up at me and just said, "Hey" and kept wiping his nose. Then my aunts boyfriend asked my mom how she was doing and she started crying again and said, "Not good" and they hugged. Of course I was upset about Gran, but I still didn't really grasp the whole thing until I saw my entire family all together just crying. I think we just hung out there for most of the day and the more it sunk in for me, the more it hurt.

I think she died from a heart attack. She was getting ready to come get me and it happened. Had it not snowed so much, the ambulance might have made it to her in time. I think about how she was ready to drive in that much snow just to come get me and take me to school. Even if she knew that school was canceled, which I'm sure she did, she was still going to come all the way over to at least watch me for the day while my mom went to work. She would have done anything for me and I would do anything to see her again and just let her know how much I appreciate her and how much I miss her. I know I was just a kid, but I wish I would have told her and showed her how much I loved her back then when I had the chance. She spoiled me rotten and I should have thanked her more and done everything I could have to spoil her. She used to take me to Baskin Robbins every Friday after school and buy me two scoops of peanut butter chocolate ice cream in a cup. That's still what I get today and always will. I never think about all the other stuff she spoiled me with though, I only remember those summers at her house playing in her backyard and watching her hang up her laundry out on the clothesline and helping her in the kitchen with her baking and cooking. I'm sure I was more in the way than anything, but she always wanted me to be there. And of course, Granny Park was one of our favorite hang outs. It's amazing to think how a lady in her sixties and a seven year old boy can both be completely happy sitting on a park bench on the side of her house doing nothing but talking.

6

1990 WAS MY first year in high school. Before school even started in August or September, I started practicing football in the summer with the freshman team. I was finally going to the school I was zoned to go so I had to start all over learning all the new faces. I don't think there were many kids that I knew at all, since most of the Pop Warner kids went elsewhere, so it was good that we all had to start getting to know each other a few months before school even started. It gave us a good chance to make friends before the senior onslaught began and we would all be pushed around for the next nine months.

We had plenty of time to get to know each other too, because we would practice in the mornings for a few hours and then go home for a while, then go back and practice again later that afternoon everyday for a few weeks. At that time, double days as they were known, were the toughest thing in the world. We did a whole lot of running and a whole lot of weight lifting. There were a lot of times when people would puke from running so much and would be so sore from lifting they couldn't walk the next day.

I somehow became a fast runner that year. Never tried to be, just all of a sudden happened. I started being one of the fastest runners on the team, so they put me in at wide receiver. I also played outside linebacker, which is all I really wanted to do, but it was fun to run really fast and go catch the ball. I became a starter at both receiver and linebacker and that helped me make friends easier, so that was good.

It's sad that it has to be that way. If you are good at something, people want to be around you and like you, but if you suck at something, people seem to ignore you and act as though they are better than you. That was my first high school lesson, everything from now on in my life will be a popularity contest.

It was great back then because this was the first time in a school I wasn't labeled as a nerd, so I soaked it all up. Especially when classes started and the other kids that didn't play football figured out that I played. They kind of looked up to the football players. Football was big at Wooster High School back then. The varsity team had won a lot of state championships over the years and just came off winning one the year before, so all of us freshman were expected to keep the tradition going and learn now so in a couple of years we could still win.

When the classes finally started, it was pretty overwhelming. There were so many people and the school was so big. The seniors looked like adults and it was tough just to find where my next class was. It was a good thing I had football friends because we all would hang out together and helped each other. It was also overwhelming at how many girls were there and actually talked to me without making fun of me. They had no idea I was a huge nerd with glasses that magnified my eyes to the size of dinner plates only a few years ago. No one knew me at all and that was kind of nice. A lot of them had known each other because they had gone to middle school with each other, the middle school I was supposed to go to, so it was a big mystery why I went to school across town. It was a big change from what I was used to school being, I was hanging out with the popular kids for the first time ever and we got to leave school for lunch, and it was actually kind of fun. The classes weren't that hard, thanks to my nerd background and every Friday we had a football game to play.

It was always a great day at school on game day. We would get to wear our jerseys to school and all the teachers would wish us good luck and all the varsity guys would threaten us so we had to win and then everyone would stick around to watch us play. It seemed like there were a hundred thousand people in the stands compared to Pop Warner and that got us pretty fired up. So did seeing all these teachers and kids in the stands that we had to go to school with. We didn't want to fumble and have to hear about it in math class or anything, so it was pretty easy to get motivated. It was a pretty good set up my freshman year. Play our game Friday afternoon, maybe go out that night, go to the Junior Varsity and Varsity game on Saturday, go to one of their parties that night, then start practice and classes all over again on Monday.

We ended up going undefeated that season and I scored a few touchdowns, so it was a good football year. Classes went ok and it ended up being my favorite year of school out of all of them. Mainly because it was all new to me and the lifestyle was all new to me. I really liked being a "normal" kid for once and not some geek who no one would talk to. All the school activities were fun, like the dances and the little pep rallies and even the seniors picking on us was fun because we knew we would eventually get to do all that. The senior football guys used to get assigned to one of us and we had to carry their helmet to practice and buy them a coke after practice and pretty much treat them like kings. I was a slave to one of the running backs that was the star player at that time. He was an all state running back as a junior, so he was a pretty big deal. Overall he was pretty decent to me and I learned some things about football from him, so I didn't complain. It was a fun year and I couldn't wait to see what would happen next year and thought it would be even more fun because I would be a big sophomore.

That summer was a good one too. My first summer as one of the guys and I went to my first party. It was right around the corner from my house and I remember my mom wasn't home so I just left and went to the party, but I didn't lock the door so I got in trouble. I was too excited to go to my first party so I was pretty hopped up and lost focus. When I got to the party it was packed with all these kids and beer. It was weird to see all these kids that were so well behaved at school and at practice, be so out of control with a beer in their hand. Of course I was an innocent young lad who didn't understand what all the hub bub was about with alcohol consumption, but it didn't take long before I finished my first beer. It tasted like crap, but I got a little dizzy, so it was good. I didn't stay long, because I didn't want to get in trouble with my mom, but once I got home, I got in trouble for leaving the house wide open anyway. The rest of the summer went pretty much the same. Football practice during the day, and hanging out and partying during the night. Those were truly good times because that's all we had to do. No jobs, no money, and no responsibilities except show up at practice in the morning. That was the good life. Sadly, that summer ended and we had to start our sophomore year.

Sophomore year was a huge disappointment. Both in class and on the field. In class, I found it a lot harder to concentrate and I think I was just too hopped up on having fun to take things like history and Spanish seriously. It's not that the classes were that difficult, it's just that I was bored with them. How can I be good at something I have absolutely no interest in? Even art class bored me to death. I wanted to draw what I wanted to draw, not look at some flowers in the middle of the room and use chalk to try and recreate their image on paper. I didn't want to make an ashtray out of clay, so of course it sucked. I did pass all my classes though, but I didn't get very good grades.

One thing that changed was we had a new principal and he changed all of the senior rules and traditions. They were no longer allowed to pick on freshman for walking on the grass or any of the other crap they used to do. It took a lot of fun out of it and now we had nothing to look forward to when we were seniors. I also wanted Arnold to have to go through all that because he was a freshman that year and I had told about how mean the seniors were to us. Although it sucked being picked on for no other reason for being new to the school, it was sad that the new principal got rid of that. School sucks and is boring, do whatever you can to make it a better experience. It seemed like people were more excited about going to school when all of that hazing and stuff was allowed and now that it wasn't, people were more excited about lunch than anything. That principal was a downer.

Junior varsity season was a downer as well. For the first time in years, the JV team had a new coach and he wasn't from the area, so he knew nothing of the tradition or type of football Wooster played. We were undefeated the year before and wanted to keep that going, but he changed a lot of players around and started a new offense, so we had to start all over again. I was still linebacker some of the time, but mostly I played running back and wing back. I really only wanted to play linebacker. The switching of players around only caused tempers to flare and soon people were arguing with each other and complaining about how they should be doing what someone else is doing and all that nonsense. I admit I was one of them, because I thought I had a chance at getting the starting running back spot instead of wing back. Running backs got the ball more, so of course I wanted that. I would always practice at that position, but once the game started, I was back to my original spot. I just didn't get it. I did get my chance though.

Our moron coach got ejected in a game for pushing a referee around, so the rules were that he was suspended for the following game. That meant that the varsity coach would coach us in that game. He was a legend in Nevada coaching. He had won more state titles than any other coach and always had offers to go to big colleges but never wanted to leave. It was kind of a big test for us, since we would be playing for him the following year, so everyone got along pretty well and played hard.

The game that week was against Hug and it was going to be the first game of mine that Turk was going to go to. I don't know why he had never gone to any others, not even Pop Warner. My mom and Gran went to every single one and after Gran died, my aunt went with my mom. It was a pretty close game and Hug was a good team, they were really fast and big. I played most of the game at linebacker and wing back but didn't get the ball until the coach finally turned to me and told me to get in there at running back. The play was for me to run to the right side. The quarterback handed me the ball and I took off and scored a touchdown on my first carry as a running back. I was pretty excited. Later in the game, I got the ball again and scored another touchdown. It was longer than the first one and I remember one of their guys chasing me and I just kicked it up a notch and he couldn't catch me. Turned out he was one of the fastest guys in Nevada, because he had won a lot of track races. I was even more excited because I knew Turk was there to finally see me play and I got to score two touchdowns. We won the game and I felt pretty good about myself passing the test and getting a chance next year on the varsity team. The following week the moron coach came back and brought back his shitty attitude with him, so after getting along and having fun for the last week, we went back to being grumpy and frustrated.

We ended up losing two games that year I think and that was unheard of for Wooster. We weren't too happy. Once our season was over with, some of us got moved up to varsity for the playoffs. That was big. I think five of us were moved up to varsity and we felt like the shit. We made it to the big time. The varsity guys were *huge* and the team and practices were so much more organized. They really only brought us up to be tackling dummies so none of them got hurt, but still, it was a compliment. Those practices were intense. I was afraid for my life the first few times those guys tried to tackle me. During the games, we didn't do anything but sit on the bench, but it was so much fun to be on the sidelines for a playoff game. The place was packed and it was loud. I wanted to play so bad, but the only way I would have gotten to play was if it was a blowout. It wasn't, but we still won the first playoff game. We had one more to win and we would be off to Vegas for the state championship. The next weeks game was against McQueen, our arch rivals and they ended up beating us and going to the state game. It sucked to see all the seniors lose their last game but it was very motivating for us to see how good we had to be next year. McQueen had beaten the varsity team the year before as well to keep us from going to state, so we had to get back on track next year.

After the football season had ended, the coaches kept trying to talk me into playing basketball and run track. I didn't want to do either, but they kept pushing me and telling me it would help with football. I thought they meant it would help with my athleticism, but apparently they meant if I didn't play basketball or run track, I wouldn't play much football either. So I went to basketball tryouts and bounced the ball and ran up and down the court like they told me to, but I just didn't like it. I liked playing in my driveway and on the hoops at a park, but organized basketball wasn't doing it for me. I think I went to one more practice and never went back. I really wish I would have gone back and played now.

As far as the track thing, I wasn't into that either, but I went and stuck with it. I really didn't care if I won or not and I'm pretty sure it showed. The first race I was in was on a relay team running the 4 x 200 race. The other three guys were juniors and seniors and I was the only sophomore. I ran the last leg of it and we were a little bit ahead of everyone when I got the baton. I grabbed it and went. Then I hear the guy next to me breathing and catching up to me, so I kick it up and really try to run fast because this was for the three other guys not just me, so I better do well. I busted my ass to keep that guy from catching me and we ended up winning by about a half of a second. I almost lost it for everyone and felt pretty stupid. Immediately after the race, the coaches started changing the way I ran. Everything from how my arms moved all the way down to my feet, they changed. So now I had to work on my new running technique everyday in practice, which made it even more difficult to get motivated to go.

The next track meet, I wasn't even close to winning any of my races. Our relay team won, but individually, I didn't. I didn't finish last though, so I had that going for me, which was nice. I'm fairly confident I would have at least been in the top three if they hadn't gotten me in my head. I was more concerned about my feet being at the wrong angle than just running fast enough to win, which is all you have to really do. I started really disliking track because of that. I never came close to winning and anytime I would run like I was used to, they would get me on it and tell me to do it their way. Maybe they did know more and in time it would have worked out and I would have been in the Olympics, but I just lost interest and got frustrated. I ran fast before and now I did not. It's not that complicated. I never won a race or even came in the top three all year and it didn't really bother me. I just went through the motions. I did end up running track for the next two years because if I didn't, I would be sitting on the bench at football games.

I don't remember exactly when, but it was sometime that year that Turk passed away. I remember being in my room and I heard my mom come home from work a little early and went to see what she was doing. I looked over the edge to the downstairs and saw her crying and asked her why. All she said was, "Turk" and I knew. He had been getting more and more sick and had lost a lot of weight. I remember how skinny he was when he went to go see me play in that game. I didn't know what was wrong with him and I think everyone just kind of kept it a secret from me so I wouldn't get too upset, but I knew something was wrong.

My aunt had gone over there to check on him and I guess she went in and couldn't find him. He wasn't in his chair like he always was, so she went out to the garage and found him laying out there. That is all I ever heard about it. For years I thought he had died from liver failure or something because he was quite the drinker, but I think he had been exposed to something in the war that finally got to him. I never asked and it didn't really matter how he died, it just mattered that Turk wasn't going to be around anymore. He was the only man that was consistently in my life and was always nice to me. We weren't really close, but then he wasn't really close to anyone. Didn't show much emotion. He was the one who got me into football and taught me all about it and taught me about all sports really. I wish he would have seen my play in more games but I'm glad he got to see at least one and I hope I made him proud. I'm glad he got to see that game and not the one where I touched the ball twice and fumbled both times. He was a good grandpa and I will always remember him sitting in his chair in his 'All American Turkey' sweatshirt, smoking his pipe and yelling at the football game on television while drinking a gin and tonic. He used to also wear a short sleeve button up plaid shirt with a pocket and I later named those kind of shirts 'Turk Shirts'. I have some and always will have some. They are very comfortable and will always remind me of him. I wish I still had his sweatshirt though.

There was never a funeral for him or Gran. I think it would have been too tough on everyone to go through that. That's all I can think of why there wasn't one. It would have been tough on me, but I do wish I would have had a chance to formally say goodbye to both of them. They were cremated and their names are next to each other at the Mountain View Cemetery. I have no idea if anyone else in the family goes and visits them, but I still do from time to time. I don't know what happens after death and if I just stand there and talk to myself or not, but it always makes me feel better to touch their names and tell them what's going on in my life. They may not hear me or may not be watching over me, but I like to think they need me to visit just as much as I need to visit them. I miss them both very much and would give anything to be back in their house having Christmas dinner. It's a shame we can't fully appreciate what we have until it's gone. I never knew simply sitting at Granny Park or riding in the Maverick to the UNR game would still be something I would give anything to do twenty five years later. We shouldn't have to lose someone to realize how much we need them around.

The rest of my sophomore year was pretty straight forward and pretty boring with the exception of me being a complete moron one time. Well, there was more than one time, but what I did this particular time was just plain idiotic.

One day after school a group of us decided to go to the Truckee River near the California Nevada state border and go swimming and hang out. I wanted to go and hang out because I knew how to do that, but I didn't want to go swimming because I did not know how to do that. I took swimming lessons when I was younger and did not do very well and even though my mom and everybody tried to teach me, I seemed to just sink. Naturally, I lost interest and before I knew it, I was sixteen years old and did not know how to swim. It was kind of embarrassing being that old and not knowing how to float, so I never told anyone and figured when we got there, I could just hang out somewhere and make some lame excuse why I wasn't swimming. So when we got there we parked on the side of the highway and everyone started to go over to this bridge. It was a bridge for trains and I just thought that was the easiest way to get down to the river. We get to the bridge and look down about a hundred feet or so and see some other people from school that we were meeting there. They were all swimming around and headed down the river. Great I thought, lets climb down there and meet up with these people. I was with three other people and the first guy looked over the edge and then jumped! He dove in and and a couple of seconds later his head popped up and he started swimming down the river where everyone else was going. Then the second guy dove in. Then the third guy asked me if I wanted to go next and I said no so he went ahead and jumped like it was no big deal. I was freaking out and thought I could just walk down after everyone was done jumping and no one would notice. But they kept swimming around down there instead of going down the river like everyone else was doing. Since I was just standing there, they all started to yell at me to jump. They thought I was afraid of the jump, they had no idea I was more afraid of the water. So they started making fun of me and telling me to hurry up and I kept telling them I would just meet them down at the big group of rocks where everyone was stopping. As I finished saying that, I heard a train. I look down and notice I am on the train tracks. Then the guys start yelling at me to jump because the train is headed right for me. I'm not only on the tracks, I'm on the tracks that are on the bridge, so I have nowhere to get out of the way. I saw the train coming and I didn't think I had time to run to the other end of the bridge to get out of the way. I started to panic. Do I get hit by the train and die or do I jump into the river and die? I decided to just close my eyes, hope for the best, and jump off the bridge into the river. I'm pretty sure I would have had enough time to run off the bridge but it was one of those moments when you have so much going through your mind you can't do anything but stand there. I remember the free fall and that wasn't that scary, but as soon as I hit the water, I got the wind knocked out of me. I sunk like like an anchor. All I remember was looking up and seeing the top of the water about ten feet above my head and kicking and swinging my arms really hard to try to get up there. I was struggling so hard and then I think I blacked out, because the next thing I remember the three guys I rode with had me on the side of the river and all this water started coming out of my mouth. I was freaking out and so were they. They kept asking me what happened and I told them I couldn't swim. They were not too happy with me. After sitting there and getting my breath back and getting made fun of for being that stupid, they asked me if I could make it down the river to the big rocks. I am incapable of learning, so I said I could. About thirty seconds into it, I panicked and the currents started taking me away and, again, they had to come over and save me. After we finally made it down to the rocks, it was time to go home. I had ruined their swimming trip. I made them feel like heroes though, so it wasn't a complete waste and I gave them a story to tell. I should have drown that day.

I have never been too comfortable around water since then. I have tried to swim and I can make it sideways across a pool, but I will not go in water where I cannot stand up and touch the bottom. Once it hits my chest, I start to panic. I always remember how scary that was to be under water and not be able to get to the top. That muffled gurgling sound you hear when you're under water freaks me out. It took a long time for me to even try to swim again and all I did was sink every time I tried, so I pretty much told myself it would just be easier to stay away from water for the rest of my life. And that's what I have done.

Junior year was very uneventful. I really don't remember anything from it class-wise. Same old stuff of trying to stay awake and get at least a B. Football-wise it was my first year on the varsity team and they moved me from linebacker to cornerback. I did not know how to play that position at all. It was completely different than linebacker.

One of our first games was against Reed I think and I lined up over their receiver and was just hoping they wouldn't throw it to him because I didn't know how to stop him. At linebacker, I was taught to read the lineman and watch where the running backs went, so I still did that. The problem with that was while I was watching the running backs, the receiver went right by me and was wide open. They threw him the ball with no one around him at all and he dropped it. I was really lucky.

I didn't start that season because all the seniors got to start and that was fine, I needed to learn how to cover a receiver anyway. My main role that year was to be a receiver on running plays. When there would be a pass play, the coaches son would come in and replace me. He was a senior, but it still kind of got to me. There was one game though where I got to go in at receiver and it wasn't a called pass play in the huddle, but because of the defense the quarterback called an audible at the line and threw it to me. I scored a touchdown and just about shit my pants. I wasn't expecting to get a ball thrown my way the whole year and now I got it and scored on my first one. That was it for me for the year and the more times I got called out of the game so the coaches son could come in and catch it, the more I got frustrated. I'm sure I had an attitude and that didn't help anything. I started just going through the motions as they say, and became a little bitter. I was still running track because they wanted me to and I was still not getting a chance to prove myself at football. I admit during the end of that season, I wasn't trying very hard. We ended up losing to McQueen again and didn't get to go to state. We only had one more year to do it. That was about it for that year.

I did make partying history that year though. I think it was that year at least. I was the first guy to throw a 'before school party'. Unfortunately, it was at my moms expense. I still feel horrible about it today. My mom was in the hospital for foot surgery I think. She had broken her foot and had to have screws put in it. I, being an inconsiderate asshole who was desperate to have friends, decided it would be a good opportunity to have a few people over. Me and a few guys started talking about it and came up with the brilliant idea of doing it Friday *before* we went to school at 7:30. Why not!? What's the worst that could happen? So I told everyone to show up around five o' clock or so. I wasn't expecting anybody to really show up except Arnold and maybe two other guys, but I think it ended up being about ten people. They brought beer and peppermint schnapps and we ended up playing quarters at six in the morning on a school day. A few more people showed up a little later and before we knew it, we were drunk and headed off to school. One of the guys girlfriends drove us all to school, so I didn't have my car. We got to school and went to our first class. Class was a lot more fun after a few shots of schnapps. As I was headed to my next class, I started seeing some of my party-mates' parents parking at the school. I knew that couldn't be good so I think I hid in the bushes or something.

Every parent that got out of their car looked pretty mad as they were walking up to the office, so I figured someone got busted and we would all get caught. I continued hiding until the next class started and I saw security walking with a purpose and a list. There was no way I was going to class now, so I went and hid somewhere else. As the next class ended and everyone started going to their next one, I asked what was going on. Everyone said they were looking for me and all the other party-goers were caught and talking to their parents. That's when I wish I would have had my car, because I would have been out of there. Unfortunately, I did not and I could not find a ride for another half hour or so. I finally made it back home and I thought I was safe.

Everyone ended up getting suspended and had to go to alcohol classes except me. When I showed back up on Monday, I was called to the principals office and got a good talking to. She called my mom while I was sitting there and I got into trouble. My mama was mad. I don't blame her, you're supposed to throw parties when your parents go on vacation, not when they are in the hospital. I was a jackass. The principal couldn't suspend me because technically they didn't catch me and couldn't prove that I was at school that day. I felt bad that everyone got suspended and had to go to drunk classes except me. I thought they would get out of it like I did. I felt even worse for doing that to my mom. That was one of the few times I got grounded.

I think it was also that year that Coach got arrested. He was still a Pop Warner coach at that time and his son went to Wooster. He played football and ran track with me and we became friends. I remember one night I went out to the movies or something and came back home around eleven or so. I walked in the door and my mom was sitting on the couch watching the news and looked all shocked and told me that Coach had been arrested for child molestation. I couldn't believe it because he was one of the nicest guys I had ever met, but I watched the news and towards the end of the broadcast, they went over their top story again, which was a local Pop Warner coach had been arrested. They showed a video of him in handcuffs getting into the police car and I just stood there in shock. My mom asked if he ever did anything to me and I said no. He really didn't. He was nothing but nice to me and he never did anything wrong and I would have never thought he could do something like that.

The next day at school was weird. Obviously everyone knew and his son did the right thing and didn't come to school that day. No one could believe it, and the mood was like if someone had died. It wasn't clear who accused him of doing those things but apparently someone came forward and told on him and everyone thought it was made up. A lot of people asked me if he did anything to me since I spent a lot of time around him and had to sleep in the same bed as him and I told the truth and said no. I thought it might be a good time to come forward about what Russ did to me though, but the more I thought about it, the more it seemed like a bad idea. I don't even think Russ had been caught yet at that time. This was about Coach being wrongly accused of something, in my opinion anyway, not about me and my problems. It was a weird couple of days after all that and we all felt really bad for his son. That must have been extremely tough on him to have everyone in the city know his dad and know what he got arrested for and have to come to school, which is cruel enough on it's own, and deal with all the questions.

Coach was later sentenced to fifty six years in prison. He was in his fifties at the time, so it was basically a life sentence. Two kids came forward and said he molested them. Who knows if it was true or not, I'm not the person to question who is capable of that or not, because I had been tricked before. I just think it's shit that he got sentenced to prison for that long with no more evidence than two kids saying he did it, and Russ was out roaming around only after a few years even though more kids were involved with him and there were actual tapes showing that he did it. The way the court system works is bullshit and needs to be changed. It is so overcomplicated that it completely rules out common sense. It is set up to protect the courts and the criminals, not the victims or the citizens. They are so paranoid of wrongly sentencing someone, they will let someone go because there might be a minuscule amount of doubt in one persons mind even though there is a mountain of evidence staring right at them. It's better to hide behind the law that was written a million years ago and no longer applies to today's world, than to risk the embarrassment of putting an innocent person away, who obviously isn't that innocent or they wouldn't be in this situation in the first place. Like I said before, they won't hesitate to lock someone up for buying or smoking pot, which doesn't hurt or effect anyone else except the government because they aren't getting their tax money from it, but they let child molesters, drunk drivers and murders go because there wasn't *enough* evidence. There was evidence, which should be all they need, but there wasn't *enough*. Bullshit.

Anyway, it was finally time for us to be the big seniors on campus. We weren't allowed to do anything to the freshman and there were no fun school activities at all like when we were freshman. That principal fazed out just about everything, so it was basically just go to school and go to class and look forward to the weekend. Again, not too much happened in the classes or in school that was very memorable. I struggled with grades because I was extremely bored with it by now, but did get good enough grades to graduate with a 3.0 GPA. Not bad at all considering the the extreme lack of effort I put into it. Socially, it was still all the same. Same people hung out together and I really didn't fit in very well with the guys from my class. I still only fit in with Arnold and his class even though they were a year younger. I just didn't want to get to involved with them because I knew I would be gone the following year and all my friends would still be in high school. So I hung out with my class as much as I could, but it was always uncomfortable for me. I don't know what it was. Maybe because a lot of the popular guys in my class didn't play football, so we didn't have much in common. They liked to always hang out together, just the guys at one of their houses. I liked to go out to a party or somewhere where there would be lots of people. Sitting around in a living room watching movies with seven other guys is fine for some people, but I was just out of place.

Towards the end of the year though, hell froze over and I got to be with my first real girlfriend. Not real like she was the first real live girl and the others were imaginary or made out of rubber, but real like an actual girlfriend to go out and do stuff with, not just hold hands with during lunch. I never had much luck with any girls in high school. I would sometimes get together with a girl at a party or something, but we would kiss and then that would be it and it would be awkward when we went back to school. If it wasn't for alcohol, I would have never even gotten a girl to kiss me I bet. I played football and everyone knew my name, but I was in no way one of the popular kids.

But I started talking to this girl everyday at lunch because she would stay at school instead of going out for lunch and once I saw that, I stuck around too. We started talking and getting along really well but flirting was as far as it ever went. Then one day after school, I was sitting in her car and all of a sudden she kissed me. It completely shocked me because I didn't even think she liked me like that. We started going out together to movies or whatever and it was going good. We both seemed happy with each other and we were together for the last five or six months of my senior year. I took her to prom and everything, but once I graduated, it was all downhill. I didn't see her much because my mom was buying a new house at that time and we couldn't move into it yet, so we were staying at my aunts which was quite a ways away. I was staying in a trailer in her side yard, so I really had no place for my girlfriend to come over. So between that and her going to summer school, I never really saw her much.

Once school started for her in the fall, it was just like being in a long distance relationship and we talked less and less. Then I found out she went to some get together at her friends house and got together with some guy. That hurt. I found out from one of the guys that was there and she told me she was just going to stay home that night. Arnold was also there I think and he was the one that confirmed it. Me and him happened to be driving and going to the mall where the guy she hooked up with worked, so I was caught up in the moment and marched into that sporting good store where he worked and told him if he ever touched her again I would kill him. I was pissed. It was one of the very few times I have lost my temper. That night, I went over to her house and told her I never wanted to see her again. I wasn't "in love" with her, but I cared about her and thought we would be together long enough to fall for her. It hurt like hell to know that someone I thought cared about me would lie and cheat on me. Once again I let my guard down enough to start trusting someone and they turn around and stab me in the back.

Besides that, football was still the main part of high school. We thought we could win it all that year. We had a good team, all us seniors had only lost three games in three years and the junior part of our team had not lost any, so hopes were high. It was also cool because it was the first time Arnold and I were on the same team. It took eight years, but it finally happened. He was a good linebacker. He had football smarts and good tackling techniques. I played cornerback again and was much better than my first outing. I started at receiver and corner my senior year, but I think I still screwed myself by not giving it my all. I knew the coaches weren't very happy with me because I didn't play basketball and didn't try very hard at track, so I kind of felt like I never got a good chance to do what I wanted to in football.

We had a good year and made it to the playoffs again. My favorite game of all time was that first playoff game against Elko. It was packed full of people and there was standing room only. It was a good hard hitting game and I only played defense the entire game, which is what I liked better anyway. I had a few tackles and I had to cover their best receiver all day wherever he lined up. He didn't have any catches all day, so I did my job. It was a close game and we ended up winning it 6-0. It was all defense and that to me is the best kind of game. The next game was against McQueen, again, to see who would go to state. Once again, we lost. It was a horrible feeling to walk away knowing our last time playing this game, we had lost. I know it's just a game, but it sure did hurt. The coaches always said we would remember that game for the rest of our lives and they were right. It was just a high school football game and my life probably wouldn't have turned out any differently had we won, but I would give my left nut to go back and play that one again and come out on top.

Every year after graduation, there would be an all star game for some of the seniors. It was called the Sertoma Classic and I got picked to play in it with three or four other guys from our team. That was an eye opener for me. They put me in at linebacker, even though I played corner for the last two years and made the all conference team as a wide receiver, but I didn't say anything. I wanted to play linebacker this whole time and I finally got the chance. We only had a week to practice before the big game and it was so much fun. None of the Wooster coaches were there, so it was a lot more laid back for me and I had a pretty good week of practice.

We all got to wear our schools helmets for the game, but because my face mask was for a receiver and had fewer bars on it, I had to switch helmets to one that had more bars since I was playing linebacker. I had to wear a Carson helmet and I'm sure that did not go over well with Wooster coaches. Not only did I not play basketball or try very hard at track, now I was wearing another schools helmet. That pretty much sealed the deal for me. There were a few small colleges interested in me to play for them and even one big one, but I'm pretty sure the coaches didn't build me up and persuaded them to change their minds about talking to me. I kept hearing how I was going to get to talk to all these people from the colleges, but it never happened. I didn't know what I was supposed to do to pursue that and no one would ever tell me, so I blew my chance. Really should have just played basketball and busted my ass at track and football.

With that, my high school career was over. Other than football, I was happy to see it end. Some people loved high school and it was the high lite of their life and they created memories that they still think about years later, but not for me. My freshman year was fun, but after that it was pretty much stupid. I did have some good times and made some good friends that I never kept in touch with, but for the most part, it was just a big popularity contest. What it took to be popular and why, I still don't know. It all seemed so important back then.

I was going to miss playing football though. It was sad to see that part of high school end and not just because I loved playing it, but because it was what my childhood had been all about and now it was ending. I had looked forward to playing every year for the last eight years and now it was over. I learned more on the field than I did in the classroom and it was always a game to me but now I was too old to play the game anymore. If I hadn't of screwed myself, I might have had the opportunity to keep playing another four years and that only made me sadder. I was really going to regret ending my football playing in high school.

I don't remember a damn thing from any of the classes that has helped me as an adult. I didn't need to know ninety percent of the stuff I stayed up all night studying and stressing over. I really didn't have to "learn" anything, I just had to memorize the names and dates well enough to pass the test. That's all school smart is, having a good memory. I think you learn by doing, not by reading about someone else doing.

So because of my 'learn by doing, not by reading someone else doing' mindset, I hated to read. I never wanted to read for any of my high school book reports. I tried, but I just couldn't get into them. Between my short attention span and the kind of books they wanted us to read, it was almost impossible for me to make it through a chapter. I just didn't like novels that would take three pages to describe how the wind was blowing. I didn't like stories in general. I liked reading about people from their own perspective and that was about it. So since I never could finish a two hundred page book in time to do the report, I started making up my book reports. I would read the back of a few books and then kind of put them all together and add stuff to make it all come together. I would then write a report on my book and make up an authors name and the title. I don't know if the teacher really knew or not but she was always surprised at my reports. She would always comment on how she had never heard of that author before and how the book sounds like it was really good. I would agree with her and that was that. I kept it going for the rest of my time in high school and never got worse than a B on any of them. I think I actually only read one book the entire four years. Sorry Mrs. Moschetti.

7

AFTER HIGH SCHOOL I did not have the slightest clue what I wanted to do. I was sick of school so I wasn't ready to go to college yet, and I had no idea what I wanted to do for a job. The only jobs I had done so far were putting files away at my moms work and picking up trash for a landlord of some duplexes. That was a horrible job. I was called a maintenance man, but it mostly consisted of me picking up trash and dirty diapers off the street. I put some boards back up on fences once in a while and twice a week I would turn the sprinkler systems on and by the time I got done turning them all on, it was time to go back and turn them all off. Then it was back to picking up other peoples garbage since they were too lazy to do it themselves. That was a fun summer job.

I knew I didn't want to do that again, but I had to do something. I really did not know what direction to go in life. Talking to the career counselors and filling out those career bullshit things in school were of no help because after answering sixty seven questions about myself and what I liked and disliked, it suggested I should find a career as a career counselor. I guess that's what people who don't know what to do with their lives do, tell other people what to do with theirs. I didn't want to do that, so I pretty much didn't do anything. We moved from our house on Randolph to a bigger house in Spanish Springs, so I had a lot of stuff to move, that was my excuse.

My mom had been in a relationship with this guy I will again name Larry, for a few years. He was a real estate guy and helped find this brand new house. My mom was doing really well and it was time to move into something bigger. We spent almost ten years in the house on Randolph and a lot happened there, but it was time to move on. It was sad to leave that house, but it was exciting to move into a brand new one. Shortly after we moved into the house is when my girlfriend and I broke up, so I really didn't have anyone to hang out with or anything to do. I was quite the loser. I didn't have a whole lot going for me. No job, no plans on going to college, no plans at all really.

Right before we moved out of the house on Randolph is when my mom got another dog. Instead of the usual big dogs we had had all my life, she decided to get a Dachshund this time. I remember this guy brought over a couple of puppies for her to look at and one of them right away pooped on the lawn and then let out a big burp and we knew he was the one for us. I started calling him a wiener dog named Lou because I thought it was funny. It stuck, but as he got older it changed to a more formal Lewis. He ended up being my best little buddy and was like a little brother in a dog suit.

So finally I had enough and started applying at some casinos because I didn't know where else to go and there were plenty of them to apply with. Not too long after I turned my application in, I got called to come in for an interview. It was my very first job interview, I felt so grown up. I wasn't very nervous because I had no idea what to expect, I just figured if they called me to come in, that must mean I'm hired. So I showed up at John Asguagas Nugget and they told me to go to the steakhouse restaurant and the manager would meet me there. I eventually found my way over there through the maze of chaos on the casino level floor and I met some short little foreign guy. I forget his name but it had a lot of z's in it and he was very nice. We sat down and he looked over my application that didn't have anything on it except high school diploma and asked me if I knew anything about being a bar back. I said no. He then asked me if I knew anything about being a busboy. I said no. He then explained what a busboy does and then asked me if I thought I would be good at it. I said yes. I was hired. Easiest job interview ever.

I had to work Monday through Friday, from nine in the morning until three o' clock or so in the afternoon. Pretty good schedule, I didn't even have to work nights because it was such a fancy place they didn't want some new busboy screwing everything up. I even got to wear a bow tie.

My first day was pretty nerve wracking and overwhelming. I had to do this whole orientation that showed me the entire casino and I was supposed to learn where everything was by the end of the week. They never tested me, which was good because that was a lot to take in for my little brain. Then it was time to learn the art of being a busboy. My instructor was a guy named Jose. He had been a busboy there for years and I couldn't understand a word he said. I finally just followed him around and figured it out. It wasn't that difficult and once I caught on, I ended up being the only busboy in the place because he went to teach more people how to bus tables. It was fine though because it was one of those fine dining places, so it wasn't about speedy service, it was about good service.

I didn't really think about my job too much, I just kind of did it. I didn't like it, but I didn't complain or anything, just kept my mouth shut and did what I was told to do, which is what I should have done in high school. I worked there for awhile and started to get to know some of the people and found it fascinating that some of them had been working there for decades. I hoped that wouldn't happen to me. I didn't know what else I wanted to do, but it wasn't that. It wasn't bad, I got free food and a paycheck and cash tips everyday, but doing that for ten plus years would have been a bit too much. I wasn't too motivated back then, but I was motivated enough to not fall into that trap.

For the time being though, it was fine. I started becoming friends with one of the waitresses there. She was about twenty years older than me, but we got along pretty well. We always had fun when we worked together and she always tipped me really good. I also became friends with the new manager of the place. The little foreign guy got promoted or something and this guy was brought in. He was really nice and laid back, so it really wasn't that bad of a place to work at all. I continued working there and over time I kept noticing that the waitress was starting to flirt with me more and more. I wasn't positive, not a lot of girls had flirted with me in my life, but I was pretty sure.

Then one day after work she asked me to go have a drink with her. I told her I would love to but I was only eighteen. She told me to lighten up and go with her. So we went to one of the casino bars and had a drink and talked. I told her all about how my girlfriend cheated on me and how upset I was over it and she just told me that everything would work out for the best. We finished our drinks, said our goodbyes and went home. A few days later, she asked me to go get another drink with her across the street at a bar. I said sure and we headed over there after work. She told me all about her husband and how much she hates him and how mean he is to her. We sat there and talked for a long time and then she asked for a ride home. Of course I told her I would, so we headed to my truck. As we were sitting in my truck letting it warm up, she looked at me and came right out and said, "You want to go get a hotel room and make each other feel better?" I was shocked and didn't know what to say at first. Of course I agreed, I'm not an idiot, and we went and got a motel room.

The next few days at work were weird but mainly because she was acting weird. A few of us went to have a drink after work again and she told us how her husband thinks shes cheating on him and he is being mean to her and threatening her and she didn't want to go home. One of the hostesses that was there offered for her to stay at her place that night. She agreed only if I would stay with her. I knew I shouldn't get involved but I went anyway. We stayed in an extra bedroom and the next day I dropped her off near her house. She was scared to death of her husband but had to go home eventually. The next few days at work, she kept calling in sick and eventually quit or got fired, not sure which. Then the manager wanted to talk to me so we went and sat down. He said he knew what was going on between the two of us and that it didn't matter to him, but she's not working there anymore and the husband knows it's someone she worked with and he is looking for him. I guess she told the manager to warn me, so he did and then suggested that I move to another restaurant in the casino for a while so the hubby couldn't find me. He was the best boss ever. He got me to go over and bus tables at the buffet working the night shift. It really worked out better because it wasn't as stuck up in that restaurant and I made more in tips, not to mention there wasn't as big of a chance of me getting killed there. I have no idea what ever happened to her and her husband but I hope she got the guts to finally leave him.

Why we stay miserable for fear of change is ridiculous. We would rather continue to suffer than to make a change to become happier. I don't get it, even if it might be difficult at the time, isn't it worth it to try and make it better? Just trying alone ought to make you feel better I would think. Just keep moving forward, that's all you have to do.

While I was working there, Arnold graduated and I think I helped him get hired at the Nugget as well. I didn't really know what his plans were after high school, he never told me and I never even really thought about it. I just figured he would go to college and try to play football, he was good enough to play so I just assumed. He just wanted a summer job, so he applied at the Nugget and got hired as a busboy. I figured he would do that until it was time to go to college, but he ended up only working there for maybe a week at the most and then he moved to L.A. where he was born and his dad still lived. I was pretty surprised because he never said anything or hinted that he wanted to move there. So he left and once he got settled in and everything, I went down there to visit. He lived with his dad in Marina Del Rey and it was really nice. I had never been anywhere in Southern California other than Disneyland, and I thought it was so cool down there. I visited a few more times and every time I liked it more and I was kind of jealous that he got to live there.

I think it was somewhere around this time that I moved into an apartment with one of my friends. It was right down the street from the Randolph house and for whatever reason I wanted to move out of my moms house. Probably didn't want to, just felt I had to. My roommate was one of my best friends and it was cool because we got along really well. The apartment was really small and my room was the size of a closet but it was the first time out of my moms house so what did I know? We had some good times and then he got a girlfriend so I ended up being pretty much on my own. His girlfriend did introduce me to one of her friends though and we hung out a couple of times but for some reason out of the blue, it ended. Don't know why, I always just assumed it was me. I was never really good at talking to girls so she probably thought I was weird or something. If I would have known that she was going to be the last girl to want anything to do with me for the next few years, I would have tried a lot harder to make it work.

I continued working at the buffet for another year or so and it was good. I met a lot of people who worked there that had a lot of different outlooks on life. Some of the people were there just for a job and so they could go to college or pursue other jobs. Other people were there because it payed the bills and couldn't afford to do anything else. Others just liked waiting tables and didn't want to know what else was out there. Those are the ones that scared me. There is nothing wrong with waiting tables, but you only get so many years to see and do other things, why limit yourself to only doing one thing your entire life. The more I saw these people everyday do the same thing at the same times with the same attitude, the more I wanted out. I couldn't get over how they didn't want more and could just keep doing the same exact thing day in and day out. These people had been doing this for years and years, I was bored out of my mind and getting antsy after a couple of months. Maybe it's just me, but the most exciting part of doing something is learning how to do it. Once I know how to do it, I want to move on. I want to know how to do a lot of stuff, not just one thing. I have a short attention span, so maybe that has a lot to do with it. So after seeing these waiters and waitresses say the exact same thing to every table, every night, I had to move on. Probably not the wisest decision without having any other jobs lined up, but I didn't think of that, I just wanted to get out before I found myself being a fifty seven year old busboy. I remember going up to the manager and telling him that I was putting in my two weeks notice. He asked why and I said I had to move on. On my last night there, we all went out and got drunk and that was that.

I worked at the Nugget for two years and I made some good tips and met some good people and some weird people. It was a good first "real" job for me. I learned a lot on how the world works and how that popularity contest that started in school continues on in the real world. More importantly I learned what I didn't want to do, even though I was still clueless on what it was I did want to do.

The more I thought about it, the more I figured I should go to college and try to figure it all out. I heard college was the pathway to success, so I thought I had to go. Turk had put some money in an account for me and I think it was one of those things where I had to be eighteen to be able to get it out, so I was going to use some of that to start going to school. I think my mom and aunt helped with the rest. In the back of my mind I also wanted to try and play football, but I had to get into a college first. I didn't want to go out of state or anything fancy like that, I just wanted a chance to play football and see what all this college talk was about. So I applied at UNR.

While I was waiting to hear if I was good enough to go there, I went and talked to one of the football coaches. I set up a meeting and everything. I went in and met with him and asked him what I needed to do and how to walk on and all that stuff. He looked at all my paperwork and said that he remembered hearing my name a few years before when I came out of high school and that they were actually looking at me back then, but never pursued it. He didn't say why, but I'm pretty sure I knew why. Those bad decisions when I was seventeen were still haunting me. He then told me I would have to take the SAT's again since it had been so long since I took them, but I couldn't do that until the end of the next semester, which was right after football season. He explained to me how once I take those and do all the right things with my college classes, I would be able to try out for the team the following spring. I was pretty excited to hear that even though it would still be another six months before I would have a chance. I thanked him and walked away.

Not too long after that I found out I did not get accepted into the UNR because I had not taken my SAT's in the last year, so instead, I could go to the Community College and take so many credits and then transfer over to UNR. And that's what I did. Now I had a reason to be motivated, I wanted to get out of the little school and go to the big one and at least try to get on the football team. I started by taking whatever classes I was told I needed to take and did fairly well in them. I tried a lot harder than I did in high school and actually studied and wanted to get good grades this time. I also started working as a laborer for Desiderio Properties, an office complex where my uncle worked. It was a little tiring to do both but no big deal.

I finished the first semester and went right into summer school because I wanted to get as many credits as I could so I could get into UNR faster. I finished up the summer school semester and went into the fall semester. I was still working for Desiderio at the time and I moved into my aunt's old house in Sparks, where I first lived back when I was two. She just wanted me to pay the mortgage payment on it, which was only about six hundred dollars and I had my old roommate and one other guy from high school who were going to be my roommates, so it only ended being two hundred dollars a month for rent.

Finally I was able to transfer to UNR in the upcoming fall semester. Of course since I would not be going there until football season was already underway, I had to wait until the following spring for a chance to try out. That sucked, but at least I accomplished something and was able to transfer to the big school with pretty good grades. I was excited to go to that school too. Community college was pretty fun, so I figured a university must be a million times more fun.

Since I wasn't able to try out for football yet, I somehow got a job at the UPS company. I saw they were hiring loaders for the Christmas season and it was just a seasonal part time job from five in the evening until ten o'clock or whenever the trailers were loaded for the night. I just wanted to make as much money as I could because I didn't have that much to go to UNR with and I didn't want my mom and aunt to have to pay for it all.

So my schedule was wake up around five thirty in the morning, go to two classes, go work with my uncle at Desiderio until four, then go work at UPS until ten, then go home and study until I fell asleep. I didn't have anything to do on the weekends, so I even cleaned the carpets at the offices one of those days. It was exhausting. The Desiderio job was physically tiring because I would spend all day carrying sheet rock and lumber or digging post holes or loading up the mess from an office being remodeled and taking it to the dump. The UPS job was more physically tiring because I would spend four or five hours straight loading boxes into a trailer as fast as I could. The classes were mentally tiring because I didn't have much time to study. I lost a lot of weight during all of that. I weighed 180 pounds before and dropped down to 150.

Working for Desiderio Properties was a good thing for me to do at the time. My uncle had worked there for about ten years or so and thought it might be good for me to learn how to use tools and do carpentry work and maintenance type stuff. He got me the job even though we didn't really know each other then. He always did his own thing and he didn't talk to any of us that much. He and my mom never talked until they got into a business together. He, my mom, and my aunt somehow got into buying a self storage place a few years before and through that, he and my mom became close and started being friends.

So I don't remember how, but he ended up getting me that job. We working for this lady who owned a lot of property around Reno and she had her maintenance guys to take care of all her office buildings and apartments. My uncle, Martin, and this other guy named Neal were the two main guys. They did all the remodeling of the offices when the renters were moving in and out and did most of the outside maintenance as well. They usually had a couple of laborers to do the dirty work and help them. That was my job. I pretty much just cleaned up after them and put stuff away and carried heavy stuff like sheet rock and garbage, but that was ok, I liked doing the physical work and it was a good place to learn. I learned how to do some minor carpentry work and some fix it things but I mainly stuck to my laborer title and loaded and unloaded things into the truck and the work place.

The UPS job would have been a lot better if it was my only job. By the time I got there I was already tired and sweaty from going to school and working all day. I had maybe a half hour between jobs and most of that was driving. When I showed up, I would go to my assigned trailer and once the packages started coming down the slide, I would scan the bar code and make sure they were the correct zip code for the trailer, then start loading them in. And I had to load them correctly, not just throw them in. There is actually a method to stacking boxes and it's a lot more difficult than it looks. I had to load them so they all supported each other and they wouldn't come loose even if you wanted them to. It took a lot of practice to get it down and the bosses would usually come around and inspect how my "wall" looked. It had to be sturdy, no spaces in between the boxes, and the front had to be as flush as possible. All of this had to be done as fast as I possibly could do it because the slide that all the boxes came down would get backed up and start overflowing if I wasn't stacking quick enough. It was stressful at first getting yelled at and looking back to see a mountain of boxes you had to scan and stack, but it was just like anything, with enough practice it became easier and I started being pretty good at it. I ended up being one of the guys that went around and helped the guys that were getting backed up because I was getting so fast at it.

College wasn't much fun for me because all I did was struggle to stay awake during class and I didn't have any social life because I worked so much. It wasn't what I thought college life was supposed to be like. The classes were really boring and I didn't really understand why we had to be in class when all the teacher did was summarize what the two hundred dollar book had in it. I don't remember a whole lot about my first semester at UNR, I think I was sleepwalking through most of it.

Going to school and working two jobs was not the right time to have two roommates. They were good guys and I wanted to hang out with them, but I was so tired I just wanted to go to bed when I got home. They would be drunk and loud and would make fun of me because I was in bed and they were out in the living room with girls or with more of their friends. It did suck to have to hear them out there having fun being normal twenty year olds while I was lying in bed feeling like a seventy year old. It was very lonely sometimes in there. I knew I was just trying to do the right thing and work and go to school, but it was really tough to hear my friends out there laughing with their girlfriends, knowing there was no chance of me meeting a girl. Having two roommates sounded like a good idea, but I felt even more alone living with people. I didn't fit in and I was crazy for thinking I could.

It was nearing the end of my first semester at UNR and it was also nearing the end of my seasonal job at UPS. I was kind of hoping to get on all year with them and thought that I had done a good enough job for them to hire me on. It was getting close to my twenty first birthday and instead of going out and getting obnoxiously drunk, I went to Disneyland with my mom. On our last day there, I stopped at 7-11 and got some chili cheese nachos before we got on the plane to head back to Reno. By the time we got back to Reno, I didn't feel very good. I spent that night and the next day with food poisoning and I had to call in sick because of it and when I went back to work, the manager told me I would not be hired on full time because I wasn't at work the day before. I was upset, but kept my cool and told him I understood and went back to loading the trailer. I kept working just as hard and about halfway through the night, he wanted to talk to me again. He told me he was so impressed with the way I handled myself and how I kept working hard, that he reconsidered and I can come on full time if I wanted to. That was cool even though I knew that was all a big ego trip to make him feel important, but I needed the job so I kept my mouth shut.

Back at Desiderio, I continued working hard as well. We were busy and I started doing more and more as I was learning. It was nice to learn how to do some of that stuff, but it was also nice to finally learn about my uncle after twenty one years. I never knew anything about him and was always scared of him, so it was nice to learn there was nothing to be afraid of and he was actually one of the funniest people I had ever met. We started getting along pretty good and I think he was kind of amazed at how I was working so much and going to school. He taught me a lot and he learned from Neal who was always teaching both of us how to do things. Neal knew how to do a lot of things but he wasn't the best teacher. He thought yelling at you that you were doing it wrong was teaching you. I learned mostly by not listening and just watching what he was doing. My uncle was a much better teacher, but they both loved to make fun of me if I did something wrong. I would get belittled until I wanted to crawl underneath a rock and cry. And I did a lot wrong, it was my first time doing any of that kind of stuff, but to them it was hilarious. That kind of put a damper on my 'go get em' attitude and I started being a little hesitant about trying to do something I wasn't sure how to do. The belittling was funny at first but then it kind of got old and I avoided doing stuff so I wouldn't get made fun of.

I continued to go to school and work the two jobs for a while even though it was really starting to get to me. Lifting heavy stuff all day and then spending the night loading boxes really started to take a toll on my back. Everyday it would hurt more and more but I wanted to be tough and just work through it. Every night after I got done with my shift at UPS, I would walk back to my truck still bent over because it made my back feel better. I was only twenty one but was walking like I was ninety one.

The days at Desiderio got a lot tougher as well. There was this little ramp that lead up to the shop and it hurt so bad to walk up that thing that it almost made me cry. My back pain had now moved down my left leg and I could not take a full step with it anymore. Then one day our job was to go put in a sprinkler system or something that required digging a trench. I remember standing in this trench scooping out what the tractor couldn't get, and finally having enough of the back pain. I decided to not go in to UPS that night because I just couldn't do it. I called in sick and told them my back hurt too much to come in. They asked if I had done it at work and I said no. I really should have said yes so I could get Workman's Comp, but I couldn't prove that I did it there. It was just a combination of the two jobs for the last few months. After a few days I went in to UPS and told them I was quitting because my back wouldn't let me do it anymore. It was sad to be be forced to leave because I was too weak, but it was one of the worst pains I have ever had. I liked that job too, but not enough to push through that kind of pain.

I kept my job at Desiderio and at one of the offices in the complex, there was a chiropractor that my uncle went to, so I decided to go and see if he could help. He tried but eventually sent me to another doctor type person and then to a physical therapist. Apparently I had pushed my back so out of line that it pushed my hip muscle sideways and it was all pinching a nerve down my leg. No wonder it hurt. I spent a long time in the therapists office getting pushed on until I wanted to puke, but it eventually got better. It still hurt to run and lift really heavy things for another year or so and that's when I finally accepted I wouldn't be playing football again. It had been almost three years since I had played and I knew it had been too long to be able to get back in it. Football isn't something you just start doing again. I knew I could keep up with the running and catching, but it was the hitting I wasn't sure of. It used to hurt to get hit after only a few months off from it, I couldn't imagine what it would be like after three years. One hit and I would be done.

That is my biggest regret of my life. I wish I would have had the work ethic back then playing football that I have now. I work my ass off now and have no excuses and I don't care what people think of me. I just keep working as hard as I can until it's time to stop. If I would have had that kind of mentality back then, I wouldn't have had to work two jobs and kill my back and wait three years for a chance to play again. I know I could have played in college if I had would have given it my all instead of my sorta. I loved the game enough, but was caught up in the attitudes of the coaches and myself. I knew the coaches weren't too happy with me and I let it get to me instead of just putting my head down and proving them wrong. There was a lot of politics involved and I used that as an excuse instead of motivation. If I would have dedicated myself to being the best player I could have been, it wouldn't have mattered that I didn't play basketball or didn't like running track. I thought it was them keeping me down but I have figured out that no one can keep you from doing anything except yourself. It's all your attitude. I had a shitty attitude back then and that's what I wish I could go back and change, the rest of it would have taken care of itself.

I continued going to school even though I wasn't going to try and play anymore and it got a little better now that I had more time to study and focus on it. I was still trying to figure out what it was that I wanted to do in life. I had been majoring in Criminal Justice but that really wasn't doing it for me, so I started taking Psychology classes and that was at least more interesting to me. The more I thought about it though, the more I wondered why I wasn't trying to get an art degree. I loved drawing and loved to look at all kinds of art and it all fascinated me. I had drawn since I was around four or five, so that must be the career for me. So I signed up for the first art class and was kind of excited to take it. Sounded great, spend an hour a day drawing or painting or whatever it was. It was going to be a much better semester than before now that I was only working one job and could concentrate better.

Back at home with my roommates, it started getting to be too much drama. I was trying to do my thing and I didn't hang out very much, one of the guys broke up with his girlfriend and started drinking and smoking pot in large amounts and the other guy was all paranoid we would get busted for it and kept yelling at the first guy to stop it. That only made them argue all the time and it got to be way too uncomfortable to be home. I don't remember what exactly happened, but I said something to hurt one of their feelings and he moved out. I think he was just looking for an excuse, but I still felt bad.

It was now just me and one other guy and it was better but I was still the odd man out all the time. He had girls over and wanted to go do stuff all the time and I couldn't get a girl to notice me if I was screaming her name while on fire, and I didn't want to stay out all night drinking with him because I had to go to class and work the next day. It finally got really awkward and I told him we had to move out. We really didn't have to, but I was planning on it soon anyway and figured I would just tell him now. He moved out and I stayed a while longer and found out that I really liked living by myself. I could come home to quiet, my food was still in the fridge, and no one was making fun of me for every little thing I did. I continued living there for a while and it was pretty nice. That's when I got my first dog.

My mom and I went to the pound and once you step foot in there, you had better walk away with a new friend or somethings wrong with you. I walked around and saw this yellow lab/Akita looking dog with floppy ears and told my mom how funny looking and cute she was. The more I walked by her the more I liked her. She wasn't all fired up and barking, she just laid there looking sad and I couldn't resist. I asked to see her outside of her cage and she was so sweet that I had to get her. I didn't even ask my landlord aunt if it was ok, which I think upset her, but I couldn't say no to that dog. In a few days I got to go pick her up and take her home. I put her in the passenger side of my truck and when I sat down in my seat and started the truck, she put her chin on my shoulder and I kissed her nose and I started to get all teary eyed. Her name was Nikki and I was very happy just living with her in that house.

My classes were going pretty good as well except for art class. It was not what I expected at all. We had to go buy all these supplies like pastels, charcoal, rulers, circle maker things and all this other stuff I didn't know what to do with. All I ever needed was a pencil and some paper for the last fifteen years. The "professor" or failed artist as I like to call him, was this little gray haired guy with a beard who also was a local news anchor and film critic, so he thought he was pretty much the shit. He knew everything and his way was the best way. Those qualities are really what you want in a teacher. Especially a teacher of art. So anyway, our first assignment was, of course, to draw the bunch of bananas on the table. It always has to be either fruit or flowers for some reason. Just once I would like to see a pile of dog crap or a live chicken in the middle of the room that is to be drawn. Both of those have lots of different shapes and textures as well, so why not?

So we use our pastels and start drawing and coloring as failed artist walks around and looks over everyone's shoulder. After seeing how horribly we are all doing, he tells everyone to stop and watch him draw the bananas. My first thought is this is why he became an art teacher in the first place, so he can get off on everyone stopping what they are doing to watch him draw. He gets up in front of the room and starts drawing these bananas and when he gets finished, I can see why he became an art teacher because it wasn't very ground breaking. I'm not saying it was bad, there is no bad art, but I did not want my drawings to look like that. That was not the style I was going for or liked. He told us our drawings should look more like his and to keep trying. His was a very impressionistic style and he told us that we didn't want our art to look like photographs because it would be a lot easier to just take a picture than to draw it. I understand that point of view, it makes sense, but why are you teaching people to shift away from their own style just because you think it should look a certain way. If I want to make mine look like a photograph, then let me. Yes it would be a lot easier to just take a picture than to draw or paint something, that's not the point. The point is for every person in the world, there is a style of art. Everyone will create something different and that's what's great about it. It's not supposed to all look the same. If you like to draw bananas that look more like yams, then fine, I appreciate that, but let me draw them the way I want to draw them and let me get as detailed as I want. As a teacher you should be teaching people how to improve at what they are already doing, not change everything they are doing and tell them to make it look like yours. You are a teacher of something that cannot be taught anyway, so stop trying. So after seeing how bananas were really drawn, we finished ours and the class was over for the day.

The next few classes went pretty much the same way. We were given something of no meaning to draw and then he would hang them all up in front of the room and critique them. According to him, there was something wrong with all of them. I thought they all looked really good and I was way out of my league because mine sucked. Those drawings were really good, but he picked apart all of them.

Everyday when we would draw, he would wander around and he would always tell me I was holding the pencil wrong. I held it like I was writing, but I was supposed to hold it like I was allergic to it or something. I had to grab the very end of it with all five fingers kind of like I was making a shadow puppet and freely swoosh the pencil around lightly and basically make a mess on the paper because there ended up being a whole bunch of lines that didn't need to be there. I amused him and tried it, but it just didn't work for me. I went back to holding it like I was writing and again he came around and got snippy with me to stop holding the pencil like that. I got snippy with him and told him it didn't matter how I held the pencil, it's what comes out of the pencil that matters. He got snippy with me even more and told me this is the class and to do what I'm told. I got snippy even more and told him I wouldn't be taking this joke of a class anymore and left and never went back.

You cannot teach art, there is no right or wrong way to do any type of it whether it be painting, sculpting, writing, music or whatever. Every kind of art came from someone creating something that had never been done before and you cannot teach anyone how to do that. I don't care who you are, your way is not the best way for anyone else but you and you only. I bet all those students in that class were or could have been really good, if dipshit didn't get them into their heads and limit them with his technique. That's what art teachers teach is technique and technique has no business being anywhere near any kind of art. All technique does is limit you from trying something new and limit your thinking about how to do it, and that is not the true definition of art. Instead of technique, teach people how to completely open their minds and not question what pops into them and go with it. That's what art is, creating an image of what is in your mind and how you see it without doubting how irrational or non-conformed it is. It's not easy to do because our overpowering egos get in the way, but that's why great artists are so rare. They don't think, they just do because in their mind, it needs to be done.

It's like with cooking. The best kinds of food come from the little diners or family owned places where the cooks didn't go to culinary school and aren't limited by how it's "supposed to be done". I'll eat the food from a southern grandma before I would eat from some fancy chef at a fancy restaurant. The grandma will come up with more original ideas and not over complicate it so much. Chicken and waffles weren't supposed to go together but Roscoe's is doing all right.

If you want to learn how to create something, don't automatically think you need to take a class for it. Having someone whom you know nothing about explain how to create will only leave you with a limited vision of possibilities. Have the wisdom of an idiot and just try to figure out how to do something without any preconceived "teachings". You most likely will come up with a way that has never been done before and that's what it's all about.

The title "artist" is one of the most over used, over abused terms there is in my opinion. Not everyone who picks up a paint brush, sings a song, or is in a movie is an artist and I'm getting sick of hearing it. It has lost all meaning. Some teenager picks up a microphone and all of a sudden he or she is an artist. Some guy who got into a movie or TV show because he wanted to be famous is all of a sudden an artist. There have only been a handful of true artists in the history of the world. Michelangelo, Shakespeare, Mozart, Van Gogh, they were artists, and it's disrespectful and ridiculous to put anybody from today's talent competitions or movies in that category.

That art class ruined college for me because now all I could see in every class was how everything was either right or wrong and there was no individuality involved in anything. I was supposed to just believe everything I heard and read and if I did that and memorized what they told me to believe well enough, I would have passed the test and would have "learned" it. I now *knew* about sociology, for example, because I memorized some definitions and sat in a classroom and didn't question the teachers perception from what he was told and memorized years before. It just seemed like all I had to do was show up everyday, not think for myself, and memorize some definitions and that would get me an education even though I hadn't actually done anything. It seemed pretty simple, but that wasn't the point. I wanted to do things for myself, not just read about them for years in college and then be completely lost when I got a job doing them.

My point is–you can't get wet from the word water. I would rather physically do something and learn that way than to jump through the hoops and spend twice as long sitting in a classroom reading about a whole bunch of stuff I won't need to know. Here's an example. A stupid example, but an example nonetheless. I learned how to put up mini blinds when I worked at Desiderio. I opened the box, got to know all the parts like the instructions told me to, had all the tools the instructions told me I needed and began reading those instructions on how to install them. I was completely lost but just did what the instructions told me to do. Forty five minutes later, Martin and Neal come looking for me and asked me why it was taking so long to hang up some blinds. I told them it was complicated because of all the measuring, marking, and drilling. They looked at me like I was an idiot and told me to watch them. No measuring, marking or drilling, just screwing in the brackets and putting the blinds into the brackets. Five minutes at the most because most of what the instructions told me to do was totally unnecessary. I didn't have to go through all those steps to learn how to do it and it would have been done faster if not for all the over complicating. That's what I feel like most schooling does. You spend years reading the instructions only to find out there is a much simpler way that doesn't require you to go through all those steps and need all those tools.

So I finished that semester and didn't go back. Partly because I was frustrated with it and partly because it just cost too damn much. My little mind started thinking about having to pay thousands of dollars every semester and I couldn't figure out why it cost so much more to go to the university than the community college. The classes were the same only smaller at the college, which was better because if you didn't understand something, you could just raise your hand and ask instead of waiting in line to make an appointment to ask the all knowing professor.

All I ever heard was I would get a better education if I went to a big university. Why? Because I would pay twice as much to take classes and buy books? Because I would be in a auditorium with hundreds of other manipulated wannabe professionals instead of a normal sized room with just a few other people who are already working and using their own money to take a class instead of using their parents money? So let me get this straight, the more money I pay to take classes, the better degree I will get, which will get me a better job? So I am buying my way into a higher paying job? That's what I got out of it at least. Why else would an Ivy League school be "so much better" than a run of the mill university and a university so much better than a community college? What do they teach about psychology at one that the other leaves out? Why don't they just all use the same books and teach the same stuff, why do only the rich kids get access to more information and get the chance to get a better job? It's the people without a lot of money that need the better job, not the ones that already have the money! I payed more to go to UNR than to the community college. I took psychology classes at both of them. They were both pretty much the same, so why is it so much better to buy a more expensive degree?

So I no longer worked at UPS, I no longer was going to school, but I was still working at Desiderio, so at least I had something going for me. Things were going good there and my back was getting better since that was all I was doing now and life was just kind of moving along. Then one day at work I was told to go back and clean up the shop with one of the other grunts. There really wasn't much going on that day and that was pretty much all we had to do all day so we took our time and before we knew it, it was done and we still had a couple more hours until we got off. So me and this other guy sat down and took a break and had a snack while we waited for Martin and Neal. As we were sitting there, Margo, the secretary to Desiderio, came by to drop something off. She was pretty much Desiderio's bitch. She answered the phones and did all the paperwork and made sure we got payed and all that. She was always very nice and nothing was different when she came into our shop. She dropped off whatever it was and then went back to her office.

A while later the boss man came back and told us that since we were sitting around not doing anything when Margo saw us, she told Mrs. Desiderio and now we were getting laid off. I thought he was joking because we had never gotten into trouble or anything before and all we were doing was waiting to be told what had to be done next. After I figured out he was serious, I freaked out because now I had nothing. I couldn't go back to UPS because they knew my back was messed up and couldn't take a chance on me making it worse, I couldn't go back to school for another few months and didn't have the money to anyway, and now I had to look for a new job without any clue what to look for. I also freaked out because it was kind of embarrassing getting laid off because I was caught sitting around. I didn't usually do that, I just didn't know what else to do, I was just a laborer, I didn't have any decision making ability. Desiderio only cared about saving money and was probably looking for a reason to get rid of us anyway, but it still shocked me and like most things that go wrong, it was really bad timing. Martin and Neal tried to talk her into giving me my job back, but there was no way. It was sad to leave because it was an all right job and I learned a lot and really liked working with my uncle. I only got paid seven dollars an hour, but it was still a regular paycheck and something to do.

I think soon after I took another trip to visit Arnold in L.A. Every time I went there I liked it more and more. The weather was perfect and I felt so much more energetic because people were all outside doing stuff and in such a good mood and it just felt like I would be happier there. We jokingly talked about me moving there since I didn't have anything else going on in my life and I thought about it, but that would be quite the commitment. After I went back home, I started talking to Arnold a lot more and was kind of seeing if it would be possible for me to move down there or not. We kept in touch but I was kind of too afraid to pull the trigger and move so I just planned on staying in Reno.

I then moved back into my moms house for a few reasons. One was I didn't have a job to pay the rent and even though it was my aunts house and I'm sure she would have let it slide until I got a job, I still felt weird about it. A second reason was now that I was living in that house alone, my aunt would come over more and complain that it wasn't clean enough or I needed to take better care of this or that. Third reason was I still had the thought of moving to L.A. and wanted to try and save as much money as I could just in case I decided to do it. The last reason was that I never felt too comfortable in that house. The only bad thing that happened in there was my dad breaking in and taking me, but it just felt like there was a bad vibe in there. Maybe it was just from that, or maybe I was just delusional, but it never did feel right. So because of all that, I moved back into my moms house at age twenty one. Didn't help my ego, but other than that, it was great. I got along with my mom really well and I loved her house and she had a bigger yard for my dog and she even had another dog for her to play with. She had gotten a Black Lab puppy named Washoe and they soon became good dog friends because they were the same age and Bandit and Bucky were becoming grumpy old seniors.

My next job was a waiter at Olive Garden. I remember applying at every restaurant I saw and the Olive Garden was the only one that called me in for an interview. I went in there so nervous because now I really *needed* a job and didn't want to screw up the interview. The manager lady was very nice and she didn't ask me too many questions and hired me at the end of the interview.

I had no idea how to take peoples food and drink orders, I only knew how to take all the dirty plates and glasses off the table after they left but I was hoping they would teach me. And they did. An entire week of nothing but training. All the new people had to take all these classes and memorize the menu and memorize all the bar drinks and learn how the food was cooked and how the computers worked and then we had to work in the kitchen cooking and preparing the food one day, then we had to wash dishes the next day, then we had to take a test, and then we finally got to go out and start learning exactly how to be a waiter. We had an opening script that we had to say to every table when we went up and introduced ourselves and that seemed so fake to me. We had to say it word for word and couldn't improvise. I had to follow around my trainer waiter for a shift and that was humiliating for me. He was a nice guy, very waiter-like where everything he says is with forced enthusiasm trying to get everyone excited to order their food, but I was so shy to begin with, that going up to a table full of strangers was terrifying. On top of that I had to memorize my script and sound believable in front of someone whose only job is to critique me.

My first table was completely embarrassing. I went up and started in on my lines, "Hello, my name is Travis and I will be your server today. May I offer you some of our house red wine?" The people said no and then the trainer waiter came in and told me to speak up. So now I am not only completely self conscious of remembering my lines, I have to worry about the volume at which I speak these lines and try to remember what the hell these people ordered all at the same time. I thought I just brought plates of food out to people and refilled their drinks. So now that the trainer waiter has ruined my flow, I forget where I left off in the script, so I get flustered and just start over only louder, "HELLO MY NAME IS TRAVIS AND I WILL BE . . ." and then trainer waiter interrupts me and informs the customers that I am new and that this is my very first table. Although humiliating, it did help. Those people were very nice and told me to just relax and that I will fine. They ordered their food, I brought it out to them, brought them more drinks and then brought them their bill without any problems. After a few more tables I was exhausted and wanted to go home. It took a while, but I eventually got the hang of it.

Once I became an expert waiter who didn't turn pale from nerves every time I approached a new table, it turned out to be a pretty good job. Good tips and it was fast paced which was good for me because it didn't give me much time to over think everything. I got to know a few of the other waiters and waitresses and they were all pretty cool. Most of them were students so it wasn't as depressing as at the casino. I became really good friends with a waitress named Sheila. Her and I would always talk and make fun of everyone else and it made going to work a lot better. She was married and had kids so I didn't even think about getting mixed up in that again, but we did spend a lot of time talking. We usually ended up staying at the restaurant late just hanging out talking until the place closed. It was nice, she was my only friend at the time.

After a few months of working there, for some reason I got a bug up my butt and made the decision to move to L.A. I called Arnold and told him and the next day he was out looking for apartments. I didn't really say anything to my mom or anyone because I knew they wouldn't be too supportive of it and I didn't want to build it all up until I knew for sure. When Arnold called me back with a place for us to move into and wanted to know if I was really ready, I said yes without any hesitation. I was ready for a change. I had no idea what it would be like or if I would hate it or what, but I wanted to see what else was out there and I had to take the chance. When I told people I was going to move there, they were shocked and asked what I was going to do there. I didn't know, I just wanted to go and see what happened. I really expected people to be a little more positive and happy for me but I heard a lot about how I was going to hate it, it was too big of a city for me, and how horrible L.A. was. I asked them if they had ever lived there and they said no, so I pretty much stopped listening after that. I really started noticing how negative people can be. No one was supportive of me moving except my aunt, which was ironic because she was usually the most negative one. She was the only person that realized why I was moving. Because I could. I was young enough to move and not have it mess up my career or anything and I should do it now, so I don't regret not doing it in fifty years. Everyone else looked at me like I was crazy and just told me I would hate it there and I was wasting my time. I didn't care though, listening to what other people think I should do hadn't gotten me very far, so I figured I should listen to myself on this one.

When I went back to work I told my boss that I was planning on moving to L.A. and asked her if I could transfer to one of the restaurants down there and she said it would not be a problem. I thought that would be perfect, I wouldn't even have to look for a job when I got down there and I had saved up enough to be able to move and get settled in for for a couple of weeks before I would have to start work again. It was all set up so I started telling everyone at work and none of them were very supportive, not even Sheila. Most of them told me how a small city boy like myself would hate being in a big city. How these people thought they knew me so well, I don't know, but I just tried to not listen to them and kept my mouth shut.

My last night there was actually really sad though. Sheila was upset that I was leaving and after work she took me out for a drink. She was all teary eyed and everything and that took me by surprise. I knew we were friends but I never expected her to cry because I was leaving. We had a few drinks and then it was time for us to say our goodbyes. She hugged me and cried, and I thanked her for being such a good friend and that was that. I didn't want to show it, but I was actually really bummed to leave her. She told me to call her when I got settled in in L.A. and I did. We only talked that one time though. I wish I would have kept in touch with her, she was a good friend.

When I told my mom I wanted to move, she was pretty upset. She didn't want me living five hundred miles away and I didn't want to either, but it was something I needed to do and wanted to do. There are millions of cities out there, how can I stay in one my whole life and not see what it might be like somewhere else? I know my mom wanted to tell me not to do it and was upset, and that was the hardest part for me. I had never been away from my mom and I felt so bad moving away, but I had to. I never went away to college and had never really been anywhere outside of Reno and just had to see what it was like somewhere else. We never really talked about it too much, because she was just really quiet when I would talk about it.

When it was time for me to go, I loaded up my truck with my stuff, my moms SUV with my stuff, and hooked a U Haul trailer up to her car full of my stuff. It was really sad to leave my moms house and my dog and I'm just glad my mom was driving down with me, because it would have been really, really hard to leave her as well. I was going to miss my dog, but I knew she would be happier at my moms house where she had an acre to run and play with other dogs on rather than an apartment with a patio in L.A. My mom and I hit the road early in the morning and as I pulled out of the driveway, I got a little choked up, but was still excited to see what would be in store for me in L.A.

8

FTER ABOUT A nine hour drive, we arrived at my new home
in Studio City. When I pulled over and found a place to park,
I saw Arnold out there waving like an idiot flagging me in and I got
pretty excited. It was a really nice place on the outside, much nicer than
I expected. I didn't really know what I expected though. It was pretty
weird to not know anything about where I was going to live and leave
it all up to someone else but I trusted him and he did a good job. He
lead us back to what I thought was an apartment but it turned out to be
a three story townhouse, with the third level being a big patio. It was so
nice I couldn't believe it. The first level was the kitchen, dining room,
half bath, and living room with a little patio out front. It even had a gas
fireplace. The second level had the two bedrooms and a big bathroom
with double sinks. The third level had a little area for storage inside but
was mainly a patio with a great view of the sunset. It was a great place
and I was all hopped up and started unloading all my stuff from the cars
and carrying it in.

My mom stayed the weekend and helped me move my stuff in and
get organized and when it was time for her to go back, it turned out to
be a lot harder for me than I thought it was going to be. She had brought
Lewis with us on the road trip and it really sunk in that I wouldn't be
able to see them anytime I wanted anymore. I got a little scared after
realizing I wouldn't have my mom right around the corner anymore. I
walked out to her car with her and she started to cry and hugged me and
that made me lose it. I felt so bad for making her sad but I also wanted
to try to make this move work and see if I could be happier. I have never
been good at goodbyes, they get me every time and this was the hardest
goodbye I had ever had to do. I said goodbye to Lewis and kissed him
on the head, hugged my mom again, and then they drove away. I stood

outside for a while just trying to gather myself so Arnold wouldn't know that I was a big baby who was going to miss his mama, but I'm sure he knew. He is really close to his mom too so he understood. When my mom got back home she called me and told me she cried for about four hours on the drive. That made me feel really bad.

When I walked back into the place it felt kind of weird. This was my new home and it felt kind of surreal. Not in a bad way, I was excited about it, but it all just happened so fast. I made the decision to move and a few weeks later, here I was. No one in my family could believe how quickly I made the decision and got a place to live and honestly neither could I, but I was committed now and didn't regret it. We spent the next few days setting up our place and in no time it was really starting to look like a home. I had saved up a good amount of money to move down there, so I was able to buy some furniture and stuff to start over with and was in no big rush to find a job. I figured if the Olive Garden transfer didn't work out, there was a million other restaurants in the city and it should be no problem at all to get a job, never was in Reno.

Arnold had moved to L.A. after high school to get into acting and he never said anything to anybody because people in Reno just wouldn't have understood that. He told me after a year or so and I thought that was great. I never knew he was into it, but I thought that was a great idea and I liked how he didn't tell everyone. The second you start telling everyone what you want to do, it's not just for you anymore, it's to build up your ego and to see how people react. I thought he would probably be good at acting, I mean that show he put on when he was seven really moved me. He started getting into modeling at first but was slowly starting to do more and more acting and always told me about the class he was in. The more he talked about it, the more I was curious about it. It sounded fun. I didn't want to become a famous movie star like he wanted to, but I wanted to join the class and see what it would be like. I figured I might as well, I didn't know what else to do with my life and maybe this would lead to some sort of job in a studio or something that I would like that I never even thought of or knew about.

He was pretty good friends with his acting teacher and after we got all moved in, we threw a house warming party and invited his teacher. During the party, I ended up talking to him most of the night and was really getting excited about joining the class. I knew I was completely wrong for acting because I was so shy, but I still wanted to do it. I decided to join the class the following week, only a couple weeks after moving to L.A. I figured if I was going to do something, do it, not just talk about it and make excuses why I haven't done it yet.

I figured since I was going to have to start paying for these classes, I should go see if I could really start working at the Olive Garden or if I had to find somewhere else to work. I looked up the nearest restaurant and it was about twenty minutes away, so I went and applied and told them my situation. They hired me on and I started working right away, no problem.

That restaurant was a lot different than the one in Reno though and I didn't like it very much. The customers were very rude and the other employees were way too good to talk to me and it just wasn't much fun. I kept at it though and just did my job. After a few weeks, Arnold wanted to take a trip to San Diego for the weekend so I went with him. I had two days off so no biggie. We went down to San Diego, hung out, and it was cool. We ended up getting back home late or something and I had to call into work and tell them I wasn't going to be there. I don't remember why I couldn't make it, but I couldn't. The next day I went into work and I got fired. I wasn't that upset, I was kind of relieved because I never fit in there anyway. Even the managers didn't talk to me or seem to like me. With that, my Olive Garden career was over.

Now I had to go through trying to find another job. I still thought it would be pretty easy, there were millions of restaurants and I had experience. It wasn't so easy. When I applied for restaurants in Reno, I would go in, get an application and return it later that day or whenever was convenient and wait to hear back. It was a little different here. I would get an application and then they would tell me when to turn it in, like the following Tuesday for example. I would go back on Tuesday and there would be literally hundreds of people there with their applications. It was a casting call to be a waiter and it took all day to wait for my turn to go talk to the manager only for him to tell me I didn't have enough experience. It was very discouraging because the people applying were all better looking and had years of experience as a waiter or bartender, so it really didn't seem like I had a chance. I continued going through the rejection process for the next few weeks without a glimmer of hope. Becoming a waiter was more competitive than becoming an actor in this town and I started to worry because this wasn't going to be as easy as I had thought it was going to be.

Acting class was emotionally draining. My first day I went in there and watched the rest of the class do scenes and then at the end, I was handed a scene to read. It was from Jerry Maguire, the 'help me help you' scene. I could barely read it I was so nervous. It was a small room with only about ten other people but still, I had no business being in there taking up these people's time. I stumbled my way through it and then had to discuss what I thought the scene was really about. I did not have a clue and just sat there with a blank look on my already bright red face.

Just like my first football practice though, I had to decide if I wanted to keep going with this or not. I thought back to how much better it got for football and how happy I was I didn't quit and I knew it was just going to take some practice and it would get better, so I told the teacher I would take the class. It was twice a week and at least it was something for me to do since I wasn't working. The next few classes got better and better and it helped that I had a good memory because it was really easy for me to memorize my lines, so that was one less thing I had to worry about. Once I started feeling a little more comfortable up in front of people, I really started to like it. I still didn't really understand everything that went into acting, but I was having fun and learning a lot every class I went to. I really started to find how much easier it was to be up in front of people when it wasn't my words coming out of my mouth. I could hide behind the lines and say whatever I wanted using the subtext and it was very therapeutic. If I had to go up there and improvise, I would have been frozen, but they were telling me what to say so it wasn't as difficult for me. It was me I was insecure about, not what I could do. I was still not very good though because I was so self conscious and was trying to make everything sound "believable" instead of being emotionally honest, but I was getting better and that's all I wanted. I really started to look forward to going to class.

It was now a few months into my Southern California residency and I was loving it. Arnold and I were having a good time and I became friends with some of his friends, a guy named Scott and his roommate, Jacob, so it was kind of like I was a normal twenty two year old who had a social life. Scott was trying to become an actor as well and had just found out he got a part in a movie. I don't remember what Jacob was trying to do but I think it was something with music. They were both really nice guys and we all used to play basketball and hang out together.

We partied a lot and L.A. was still new to me so everyday was like a new adventure and it was great.

Then one day Arnold found out that he was getting a part on a soap opera that was filmed in New York. He obviously had to take it, that was the whole point of what he was doing, so he planned on moving. I was very happy for him but a little worried about what I was going to do. I didn't even have a job and was going to have trouble paying just my half of the rent, let alone the entire thing and I had only lived in L.A. for about three months and now he was leaving. Luckily, one of the girls he had been hanging out with needed a place to live and decided to move in with me, so I still only had to pay my half. I didn't know her very well, but I didn't care, I needed a roommate. Arnold took off to New York and she moved in and it was cool at first, but we started getting on each others nerves. We argued a lot, but for the most part we just started ignoring each other.

My job search finally paid off because I was hired at the Home Depot in the San Fernando Valley. I thought that would be a good job too, something different and I figured it would be a good steady job until I could find something else. My first day, I showed up and went through the orientation and was expecting to be shown where everything was and how the store was run. Instead I was thrown out into the store with a giant 'In Training' button pinned to my chest and was told to walk around and when a customer asked me something, I was to take the customer with me and go find someone who had worked there for a while and stand there and listen to them answer the question for the customer. That way I could learn from everyone in every department. I thought that was stupid but did what I was told. The first five customers that asked me a question yelled at me because I did not know the answer and I ended up dragging them around the entire store with me trying to find someone to help *us*. I spent a lot of time apologizing.

I had to continue that routine for the next few days until I was ready to start in my assigned department which was paint. I couldn't wait to get to the paint department because I got to stay behind the counter all day and not walk around and get asked questions. That was a ways away though. I still had to complete my training and it seemed to be getting more lame by the day. We had to be in the break room a half hour earlier than our scheduled time so we could 'get to know our associates' and we had to do a lot of 'team building exercises' They were very high on the

Home Depot spirit and I could not bring myself to be that excited over a job where I had to show people where the plunger department was.

The managers there were like male cheerleaders and they expected us to have the same attitude. I tried and faked it enough to get by, but when they got us all together in a room and made us do the Home Depot Chant, I had to know when to say when. I wish I could remember the chant, but I used a lot of effort to try and block it all out. Every morning before our shift we had to do the chant and get fired up to go sell nails. I wanted to cry. I wanted to stay with it though since jobs were hard to come by and after about four good shifts, my truck died. I now had no way to get to work and it was a good half hour away and I didn't know the bus system well enough to be able to get there in such short notice. My roommate gave me a ride the first morning and one of the guys that worked there gave me a ride home that night. I somehow found a ride the next morning but could not find a ride home after my shift. I called everyone I knew and no one could get me, so I started walking. It was the middle of summer and it was hot, but about four short hours later, I made it home. It was a long way and I only knew how to get home using the freeway, not all the surface streets so I got lost a few times and probably ended up going the longest way possible. I made it though and was exhausted.

I couldn't find a ride to work for the next time and I wasn't about to walk, so I didn't go. I tried taking the bus the next time but ended up in some other city miles away from where I was supposed to be, and by the time I would have gotten back on track and made it to work, I would have been three hours late, so I didn't go. They never called me and I never called them, so technically I wasn't fired, but with that, my long Home Depot career was over. I made about a hundred and eighty dollars that week and didn't learn a damn thing except a chant.

Back at home I was not getting along with my roommate. She was even moodier than me and that didn't work. I was starting to panic because I was running out of money and didn't know what to do so I'm sure my attitude wasn't helpful to our friendship. We ended up not talking at all and that was for the best. I remember how upset Arnold was when he heard we weren't getting along. He felt bad that he got her to move in with me and now we hated each other, but it wasn't his fault, it was mine. I wasn't too easy to live with at that time and I admit it. I would have stopped talking to me as well.

Even though I didn't get along with my roommate, I was still hanging out with Scott and Jacob a little bit. I went to the gym with Scott everyday and Jacob would come over and hang out from time to time, so I still had at least two friends.

Next came another job that didn't quite pan out the way it was supposed to. I got hired at a Chinese restaurant in Studio City named Chin Chin. I was hired to work the take out section and I had to work there for a certain amount of time before I got my chance to become a waiter. I mainly answered the phone and took peoples orders. I had to answer the phone by saying, "Chin Chin Studio City, this is Travis how may I help you?" I said that about twenty seven hundred times a week. I had to wear white jeans, white shoes, and a white Polo shirt and when I came home and my roommate asked me where I got a job, I told her the insane asylum and I had to wear all white because colors scared them. She believed it so I went with it. I don't think she ever really found out I was kidding.

I worked there for a while and it was all right. There were three managers and one of them did not like me. I don't know why, I never did anything to him, but he despised me for some reason. Other than him though, I liked the people and I made some decent money in tips and I was looking forward to becoming a waiter there. Then Arnold was coming back to town to visit and we were going to Vegas for the weekend. I had my normal two days off and I traded shifts with someone else so I could have a third day off. I got it approved by the managers and everything so I wasn't worried. The next day we took off to Vegas and did the usual Vegas thing, so I don't remember much of it. When I came back to work, the manager that didn't like me called me into his office and fired me because the person that switched shifts with me was late, so it was my responsibility. I knew that was bullshit, but there was no way I could have changed his mind. He didn't want me there for a reason only he knew, so there wasn't much I could do. The L.A. job scene really wasn't working out for me very well.

Acting class was all I had going for me at the time. That was my escape and that was the only consistent thing I had in my life. I really liked all the people in class and even though the class went for five or more hours some nights, I kept wanting to do more. I usually had two or three scenes to do and although I was nervous as hell to do them, once I got up there and started, all the nerves went away. I knew I was getting more comfortable up there, but I was really kind of shocked at how everyone was telling me how good I was getting. I was slowly starting to gain confidence and I started to believe I could do this.

I was nowhere near ready to start auditioning for real acting jobs, but since I had no other source of income, I had to at least try. Arnold hooked me up with his manager and I got pictures and he started sending them out trying to get me auditions. My first audition was like my first everything else:humiliating. It was for a soy sauce commercial and the director and everybody auditioning people were Asian and I couldn't understand them very well. I had no idea what I was supposed to do. I sat down at this table in front of the camera and there was a piece of paper and an ink bottle in front of me. They just kept pointing at the piece of paper and the ink and shook there head yes. I saw a big logo for the soy sauce on the table as well so I just started drawing that with the ink. All I got was dead silence followed by a thank you. I never found out what they wanted me to do, but I'm pretty sure I wasn't even close.

My second audition went fantastic. I showed up, waited for about a half hour, went in front of the camera, said my name, and left. When I got back home, the manager guy called me and told me I got the job. I was shocked. I didn't do anything, how did I get the job? Was I the only guy that showed up? I was told to show up next week for a music video shoot. I had no idea why they picked me, but I didn't complain.

I showed up at sunrise and they put some make up on me, put a different shirt on me, and told me to just wait around until they were ready for me. I still didn't know what I was going to do. I didn't even know whose music video this was but it was quite the production. Looked like a movie set and I just walked around and was amazed at all that went into making a video. I watched all the people behind the scenes like the camera guys and lighting guys and figured I could do that and I should try to get a job doing that. I had no idea how to get into that, but I could figure that out later.

Then it was time for my first "scene". I was a paparazzi guy who kept following this rapper. I didn't know who he was, but he was pretty good. As he got out of the limo, I was supposed to take a million pictures of him as he walked up to the front door of this hotel and I nailed it. I really gave a high energy performance and gave new meaning to name actor. Seriously though, I didn't screw up and no one said anything bad, so that was successful to me. We then went inside the hotel and I followed him around some more and took pictures of him and I guess I did my job well enough because no one ever said anything to me. After a sixteen hour day, I went home and chalked up my first acting gig.

It wasn't too long after that I signed up to be in an extra casting agency. I figured they always needed people to be in the background and I was good at being in the background so it was a win-win situation. It took a while to get a job because everything in L.A. was competitive, but I eventually got a two day job working on a Jim Carrey movie. It was called 'Man on the Moon' and he was playing Andy Kaufman. The first day I worked was at the Comedy Store and I was just a guy in the audience when he was playing one of Andy Kaufman's alter egos who was a stand up comedian. It was a pretty fun day even though I didn't really have to do anything but clap and smoke fake cigarettes. Since it takes hours and hours to set up in between scenes, it got kind of boring but that's when Jim Carrey came out and started to do his stand up routine for us just to keep us entertained. He did impressions and sang and it was great. I was getting paid to be at one of his shows and it made the time go by really fast. I got off at around eleven at night and had to be back at five in the morning, but I couldn't wait. It's not like I was working hard or anything. The next day was outside of the Comedy Store and it was all about him getting out of the limo and going into the building. Why that had to take all day and most of the night to film, I don't know, but I didn't care, the longer I got to be there, the more free food I could pack in. I got to meet Danny DeVito, Courtney Love, and Jim Carrey that day and it was pretty cool. I'm sure they all remember meeting me as well.

After that it was pretty hard to find work. I was still applying at every restaurant I passed and still no calls. It was getting close to the end of my year lease and my roommate was going to move out and there was no way I could afford to stay there by myself. I had no clue what I was going to do. I kept looking for work and kept getting shot down. My account was getting really close to zero and I only had a month to figure out what I was going to do. My roommate was moving across town and I helped her move since I had a truck. I parked out in front of her new place and was moving stuff in and when I went back out to go back home, my truck wouldn't start. I left a note on my truck that said it wouldn't start, in case they tried to give me a ticket or something and got a ride back home.

The next day I got a ride back there and was going to jump start my truck to see if that would work. As we came around the corner, my truck was gone. I had no idea if it got stolen or towed or what, but it was gone. I didn't know what to do first, who do I call? What do I do? Am I just on the wrong street? I ended up calling every towing place in Southern California before I finally found the one that took my truck. They said I was parked illegally but I read the sign and it seemed fine to me, it didn't say anything about getting towed. I was pissed but had to be nice since they had all the power in that situation. I went over there and used my credit card to bail my truck out of jail and then they jump started it for me and told me I needed a new battery. I took it home and parked it *legally* in the parking garage and tried to figure out how I could get some money to buy a new battery. I had a Sears credit card and I was hoping my truck would start just one more time so I could get to the store to get the battery but of course it didn't. I couldn't find a ride so I put on an empty backpack and got on a bike and headed to Sears. I thought it was going to be a little bit easier than it was. Batteries are heavy and very awkward when they are in a backpack and you have to try to keep your balance. The tires on my bike were flat which didn't help and it took about an hour and a half and a thousand calories to get back home. I put the battery in and the truck fired right up. Then I took a nap.

It was now decision time. My lease was up and I knew I wasn't going to try and stay there, there was no way I could afford it, but I didn't know where else to go. Arnold was going to be in New York for another two years and I didn't know anyone else to try to move in with. Most people would have gone back home where their family was and admitted they couldn't make it and play it safe, but not me. I was too stupid for that kind of thinking. I loved L.A. too much and didn't want to leave after only a year. I knew I could get back on track eventually, I just needed a job that I wouldn't get fired from. I didn't think that was too much to ask. So instead of packing my stuff up in my truck and heading back to Reno, I used my credit card and got a storage unit and packed my stuff into that. I remember Arnold came back to visit and he helped me move some of my stuff and he couldn't believe I was just going to put all my stuff in there and live out of my truck. I couldn't believe it either, but I was stubborn.

After all my stuff was in there and Arnold went back to New York, I had maybe a day left in my home. There was still stuff all over the place because I didn't have room in storage to put it all in there and I felt bad leaving the place in such a mess, but there was nothing I could do. I slept on the floor that night and woke up the next day, turned in my keys, and was ready to start my life as a homeless person.

9

I DID CATCH A break right before I was going to sleep in my truck though. My acting teacher had a friend that needed someone to house sit and take care of his cats for a week, so he let me do it. It wasn't anything too difficult and I didn't get paid, but I had somewhere to sleep for the next week.

It was weird not knowing what the hell was going to happen to me. I tried to keep calm but I went out with Scott and Jacob one night and drank a little too much and lost control a little bit. It all came crashing down on me all at once and alcohol didn't help my depression. I was a wreck that night and started wandering into traffic on Sunset Blvd. Jacob made me sit down and all I did was cry and freak out. I thought I was going to be able to handle all this and bounce back, but I was only two days into it and hadn't even slept in my truck or in the park yet and was having a nervous breakdown. I was finally smart enough to stop drinking that night and the next day I felt like shit and the depression really took over. This is when I started writing. I had nothing else to do and needed to try and get it out of my head and onto paper to see if it looked as crazy there as it did in my head. I started writing a journal type thing of everything that had happened since I moved to L.A. It was nothing very exciting, just the facts, but the more I wrote, the more it felt better to write what I was feeling and what I thought about things. It ended up only being a couple sentences but I felt better after putting them down and I started to write down everything I did everyday. I didn't have much to write about other than looking for work and I started writing about how lonely I was and how I wanted to write about something so bad, but didn't have anything to write about. The more I did that, the more I found myself writing about how depressed I was. Everyday was mentally draining for me and the anxiety of not knowing what was going to happen after I was done house sitting, was getting to me. I didn't really have any close friends or anybody to talk to so writing and acting class were all I had.

My house sitting gig was up and now it was time for me to truly be homeless. I slept in my truck in front of my old house the first night. That was very depressing but it was an area I knew, so I felt safe. I only had a Toyota pickup with no camper shell and all my clothes were piled up in the passenger side and there was just enough room for me to lay against them and try to sleep. I didn't sleep much that night and the next day I went to the gym and showered and then went to a park and slept there during the day. I had gotten a gym membership when I first moved there and paid for a three year deal, so at least I had a place to shower so I wouldn't smell like a homeless man. I didn't work out while I was there though because that would only use energy and make me even more hungry than I already was and I didn't need that. The people always looked at me kind of weird because I would just come in and shower and then leave. No one said anything though.

For the first few days, that was my routine. I couldn't sleep very well in my truck at night, so I went to the park and slept during the day. I didn't stand out as much as if I had slept there during the night and I think it was illegal to do that anyway. If I wasn't sleeping, I was walking. I didn't want to drive because I would use gas, so I walked everywhere. I just wandered around and looked for places hiring or just hung out and people watched. The longer I was homeless, the more I liked to people watch because all the simple things they did looked so nice and so taken for granted. Like a cup of coffee. All I wanted was to be able to buy that four dollar cup of coffee and sit there and drink it without freaking out about everything. Everyone looked so happy and carefree walking around with their shopping bags full of stuff they didn't need.

I was still going to class twice a week and because of my recent developments and the depression that went along with it, it was helping my acting. I was so frustrated with my life that I got to let go and show it during some of my scenes and I didn't care what anyone thought anymore. I was at rock bottom, so what difference did it make if I made a jackass out of myself? I just let go of my self consciousness and concentrated on using acting as therapy. The only problem was I didn't have the money to pay for the classes and I thought I was going to have to quit and that was the last thing I wanted. I told Gary, the teacher, that

I could not pay him right now and he said to not worry about it. I asked him why, because there had been a few people before that had to stop going because they couldn't pay and he told me I was getting really good and was getting too close to really 'getting it' and I made the other actors better. That was the biggest compliment I had ever gotten I think. I was shocked and flattered. I promised I would pay him back everything I owed and after he found out that I didn't have anywhere to stay, he and his girlfriend Kate let me stay on their couch from time to time. That was another reason I looked forward to class nights, because I got to stay on their couch those nights. I was really glad he let me stay in the class because I was loving it. I still didn't have much of a desire to audition and try to find work as an actor, I just loved being in class and doing scenes and it was very therapeutic for me.

Then one day out of nowhere, my pager went off. It was 1999, pagers were the thing then. It was some number I didn't recognize and I called it back. It was a lady from the Los Angeles Zoo wanting me to come in for an interview. I didn't even remember applying there but of course I agreed to come in. She told me to come in the next day and that they were hiring for a few different positions. The next morning I was excited and took an extra long shower at the gym and made my way over to the zoo. I went into the offices and was told to go back further and meet Kayla the manager. I found her office and she was on the phone so I sat there uncomfortably until she finished what she was doing. She was a very nice lady and didn't ask me very many questions, just told me what the job was and asked me if I was interested or not. I of course said yes and just like that I was hired. I later found out she hired me because I had nice teeth. Sometimes it's all about your resume and sometimes it's about much more than that.

I was told to come in the next day at eight o' clock in the morning and I would be working at one of the churro carts in the zoo. Didn't sound too exciting but I needed a job, didn't matter what it was. I showed up a little before eight and went where I was told to go and stood there and waited to be told what to do. I waited and waited and then finally some Mexican guy pulled up on a golf cart. I asked him what I was supposed to do and he didn't know so he just told me to get into the cart with him and I rode around with him until we could get a hold of the boss and found the churro cart I was supposed to work behind. They showed me how to cook the churros and dunk them into the sugar cinnamon mixture and how to organize my cart and then left me there.

When the first customer came up to me and ordered two churros, cotton candy, two pretzels and three sodas, my head almost exploded because I didn't have a cash register or anything, just a money belt and I had to add it all up and then count back the change all in my head. I was never good at math and this was way to much for me. It took me about five minutes to figure out how much change I was supposed to give back and I still think I got it wrong. It was a lot to take in for a simple little guy such as myself.

It was a pretty slow first day though and that was a good thing and I turned in my money, asked a few questions, then got in my truck and hung out in the parking lot. I had nowhere else to go and it was still only like five o' clock so I just sat there listening to the radio. That was the toughest time for me to be homeless. What was I supposed to do with myself? I didn't have anywhere to hang out other than my truck and I had no money to go get coffee or anything, so what was I supposed to do until it was time to sleep? I usually just ended up parking in some neighborhood and walking around for hours. I sat around at a park a few times but that didn't work out too well for me. Weird people hang out at parks and they always wanted to talk to me or would hassle me. I did find a park in Santa Monica though that was primarily homeless people and no one really bothered me there. I actually slept there a few nights and it was scary at first, but I got used to it. It was a good place to hang out after work because no one would bug me and it was in a good part of town and I could just lay there and write or read or whatever until it was time to sleep. The only bad part was it was all the way across L.A. and it took forty five minutes and a lot of gas to get there. I didn't really mind it too much though, driving ate up some time at least.

Even though I did sleep out there a few times, I always felt better sleeping inside my truck. It wasn't very comfortable at all, but at least the doors locked and it felt like I had some privacy. There was only one time I was bothered in my truck. I had parked around the block from the park and fell asleep in my truck. All of a sudden I was woken up by some guy knocking on my window yelling at me. I just about pooped my pants and started the truck and took off. After that I was really careful about where I parked and started covering up my windows when I slept so no one could see in.

The zoo was going along fine and I was getting better at counting out change and not burning the churros. It was pretty boring standing there all day, but it was a job so I couldn't complain. After work I started going to bookstores instead of hanging out at parks. I thought that would be much more productive and most of the stores were open until eleven, so I had a place to stay where no one would bug me. I was never much of a reader, but I started reading a bunch of acting and directing books and tried to get as much out of them as I could. They were entertaining but didn't really help, because as I said earlier, you can't learn by reading about doing something, you have to actually do it. I also started reading poetry books. Charles Bukowski was my favorite and I think I read all of his books. I started reading everything, no matter how random it was. I went from reading Pablo Neruda to reading about the theories of Albert Einstein.

I then found Henry Rollins. I knew of him from Black Flag, but I never knew he was a writer as well. I read one of his first books and was hooked. All the loneliness, depression, and frustration he was writing about, was exactly how I felt. I read every book of his and then when I had enough money, I went back and bought them all. I have every one of his books and I always look forward to when his next one will come out.

Every night I would go to the same store in Studio City and spend a few hours in there. I think they got kind of sick of me always hanging out and not buying anything though, because they told me they were going to start charging me rent and they didn't seem too amused. That's when I thought it would be a good time to change stores for a while. I ended up going all the way over to the bookstore in Santa Monica. It was a lot bigger and it was easier for me to hide in and I always just felt more comfortable in Santa Monica. I continued to read everything and anything and it made the time go by quick.

I still slept at the park on my days off and I really enjoyed watching all the other homeless people that were there. I ended up talking to a lot of them and they all had different reasons why they were homeless. Some were just too crazy and this was it for them and some were trying to get back on track, but just couldn't get their shit together enough to do it. Some were addicted to drugs and alcohol and that's all they cared about and some were professional panhandlers. Those people made more money than most business owners. They had a good thing going and didn't care how pathetic or immoral it was to beg for money. From what they told me, most of them started out just asking for money because they needed it and were trying to get their life back together but once they saw how easy it was to just ask for money and not have to do anything for it, they were hooked. Why go work for someone else when they were getting good money now and didn't have to answer to anybody? A lot of them would just rather live that life and some of them even had houses and everything.

Just about all of them would ask people for money because it was so easy and people would give it to them. If we really wanted to stop homelessness, all we would have to do is stop giving them money. If we keep giving them money and shelter for free, they will keep taking it. Just like us with our jobs, we keep going back to a job we don't like just because it gives us money. We stop getting our paychecks, we stop showing up and are forced to go look for something else. I know people come across hard times and that sucks, but everyone has the capability to get themselves out. They need to do it on their own, not have someone do it for them or they will fall right back down again and expect to be rescued again. It sounds rude and uncaring, but people need to take responsibility for themselves.

I never once asked for money or change. I never dug around in garbage cans to find aluminum cans. I never had a shopping cart and I always shaved. No one at work knew I was homeless. I worked there for a couple of months before I finally slipped up and told someone. The word got out and my boss found out and offered for me to stay with her. I didn't really want to, but she insisted and I figured it would be nice to have a couple of nights indoors for a change so I said yes. She lived in a trailer park in Bell and it wasn't the safest feeling neighborhood, but who am I to be picky? I had my own bed and everything and it was my boss, her daughter, and her two year old grandson that lived there. It was very awkward, but it sure was nice to sleep in a bed. I stayed there a couple of nights a week and stayed with Gary and his girlfriend on class nights and the other nights I would sleep in my truck or on the beach. I found a spot on the beach by the Santa Monica Pier where I could sleep all night and they wouldn't kick me out and that was a lot better than the park. That was my routine for a while because I didn't want to be in the way or burden anyone by staying at their house all the time.

My boss at the zoo also had a lot to do with the hiring at Dodger Stadium. I think it might have been the same company that provided people food for the zoo, so she asked me if I would like to work at the stadium when there was a home game. I said yes and before I knew it, I had two jobs. I would work at the zoo during the day, then go sell hot dogs at the game at night. It ended up being about fourteen hour days, but what else did I have to do? It was a pretty good job and I was always busy so time went by fast. All I did was work behind the concession stand selling beer, hot dogs, nachos and whatever else people wanted and when the game was over, I was off. I got paid by the day not the hour so it was nice when the game only went three or four hours. I worked there the entire baseball season and it was a pretty relaxed job.

Back at the zoo I was promoted from churro cart guy to the delivery guy for all the churro carts. I got to drive around in a golf cart and stock all the churro carts and burger stands in the zoo. That job was a million times better and I even got a walkie talkie so I was pretty much a big deal. I ended up getting more hours as well. I would get there early in the morning and pull all the carts from the garage to their spots in the zoo and then stock them with churros, sodas, pretzels, and all that. On the weekends we usually had about seven of those carts around and it took a few hours to set them all up and then I would be driving my golf cart around restocking them all day and then had to break them all down and put them away at the end of the day. It was a pretty fun job because I got to drive around so much and didn't have to deal with any money.

Weekends were always busy but during the week it was really slow and I thought they might cut my hours back, but instead they asked me if I wanted to learn how to drive the tram and if I did, I could do that during the week. I agreed and that was my new job. I drove the tram during the week, was churro cart stocker guy during the weekends, and worked at Dodger stadium a few nights a week or whenever there was a game. I was also still going to class two nights a week so I was pretty busy. I was slowly starting to save up a little bit of money and finally got my account out of the negative twenty six dollar range and was starting to feel a little bit better about myself. I was really getting tired of sleeping in my truck and on the beach though, so I started to stay with Gary and Kate more. They were very nice and told me I could come over anytime, but I didn't want to be in the way so I would usually wander around or go to the bookstore until it was late enough where I could just go over there and sleep on their couch and wouldn't be in the way.

It had been a few months now that I had been homeless and it wasn't getting any easier just more tolerable. I knew my spots I could go and not be bothered and was getting used to walking around on the streets for most of the night. I did a lot of walking. I used to just walk around the neighborhood where Gary lived and just look at everyone in their homes and it looked so nice. I wasn't peeping, but I glanced as I walked by if their window was open. It was all the simple things I wanted to do like lie on the couch and watch TV or sit on my porch or cook dinner in my kitchen. I never knew how good I had it until I didn't have it anymore. I spent hours every night just walking and thinking and hoping I could save enough money to get a place to stay. I was over thinking everything and was worried I would become one of the crazy people that would walk around and have conversations with themselves and then lick their arm and smell it. It didn't seem that far fetched because I was really wrapped up in my own head. That's when I really started getting into writing. That and acting were the only things that made me feel better so I started writing not only about what I was doing but more along the lines of what was going on in my head and that seemed to take a while. I was frustrated with not having anywhere to live, I was so lonely it hurt, and I just felt like such a loser. I started going to the coffee place and sitting there and writing. I could finally afford a cup of coffee and I loved hanging out there and writing because it was crowded enough where it had the energy to get me motivated but not so crowded I couldn't concentrate. And it made me feel like I had a social life because I was a regular and they knew my name and thought I was some professional writer or something. Little did they know I was just some homeless guy who worked at the zoo and was writing down all of my depressing thoughts and feelings so my head wouldn't explode and had no where else to go. Going to coffee became my favorite activity and I would spend every night there and every day off I had there.

I remember a couple of times a week I would go to the pay phone on Santa Monica Blvd. and call my mom. She never said anything but I could always tell she was worried sick about me. She wanted me to just move back home but I still wasn't ready to do that. It would have been a lot easier to do that, but I wanted to see if I could make it all work and I really did love being in L.A. even though I was having a hard time.

Those phone calls really helped me make it through. It was good to hear what was going on back home and how well my mom was doing and hear about the dogs. It just made me feel like everything was going to be all right. That's what moms are for. I do feel bad I put her through that stress though.

Things were going good for the most part but I was feeling really bad about staying with Gary all the time so I thought I would save up and once or twice a week I would get a motel room. I thought it would be a good idea and I could have my own space and get out of other peoples homes for a while. I couldn't afford to stay at a big name motel 8 or anything so I just stayed at some dump in North Hollywood. I went and got the key and was all excited to have a bed and a shower and be able to just relax for the night. I walked over to my room and opened the door. The smell of Pine Sol just about made me pass out and the first thing I saw was blood splattered on the wall. It had been there a while and they tried to cover it up but it was still noticeable. It was that orange-brown color and started at eye level and went up to the ceiling. I thought about leaving but it was raining out and it was too late to find somewhere else to stay and I was really tired. I took the bedspread off the bed and laid down and watched TV for a while then turned the shower on. It was gross in there too, but at least there was hot water. I got out and turned the lights off and went to sleep. Around two in the morning I was woken up by the people next door arguing and fighting. He was screaming at her and she was throwing stuff at him and they were very loud. I just wanted to sleep and they kept banging against the wall and I think he was beating the crap out of her. It finally stopped and I got a good two hours of sleep before I had to go to work. I'm pretty sure there was blood splattered on their wall after that night as well.

My living arrangements pretty much stayed the same for the next few months and so did my routine. After work I would go sit at the coffee place and write or read until it was time for me to figure out where I was going to stay that night. I stayed with Gary and Kate most nights, so I would drive over to Santa Monica and find somewhere to eat and hang out. A lot of times I would just go to the Ralph's and buy a sandwich and chips for dinner and go eat it on the beach. Then I would either go to the bookstore or just walk around the neighborhood until it was late enough that I could just go over and sleep on Gary's couch and not be in their way all evening. If I didn't stay with them I would stay with my boss once in a while or just sleep in my truck or on the beach. Then sometimes on my Friday night I would treat myself and get a motel room. They were never very nice rooms, but it was somewhere I could take a long shower, watch TV and not feel like I was in anyone's way. There wasn't any blood stains in any of them, so it wasn't that bad. I also got to sleep in and hang out until check out time at eleven so it was nice have a few more hours of a roof over my head.

Arnold was doing well on the soap opera and he even got nominated for a Soap Opera Digest award for best newcomer. The awards were held in L.A. and he invited me, Scott, and Jacob to go. We all got dressed up in our suits and headed over to Universal City where the award show was going on and it felt so weird for me. I was surrounded by all of these rich, successful people, Arnold was a soap star now, Scott was in a movie that was going to be coming out the following year which ended up being a very popular movie, and here I was some homeless loser in a suit that didn't fit right, packing in as much free food as I could because I couldn't afford to buy my own. I felt very out of place but that feeling seemed to be happening a lot. Everywhere I went I felt out of place. I'm sure it was just in my head, but it felt like everyone knew what a loser I was and was laughing at me and I felt like I was being stared at and criticized all the time. I started to get sweaty and panicky anytime I would be out in public and I felt like I just wanted to run away as fast as I could. It was the same feeling of wanting to get away from my dad but not being able to. That claustrophobic feeling that made it feel like my heart was going to explode out of my chest.

I was pretty shy to begin with, but now that I was completely uncomfortable in every social situation, I talked even less. When I did talk, it usually came out wrong and made me feel even more stupid and sweaty. I kept my mouth shut as much as possible and I was always criticized for being so quiet. That only made me feel like more of a freak. I found myself constantly apologizing for myself. I wanted to talk more and be more social, but it was just so terrifying to be put on the spot and have all the attention on me that it just felt safer and less embarrassing to be quiet. I liked being around people, I just wanted to be a fly on the wall and have no attention on me and just be able to listen to everyone else.

My panic attacks were an accumulation of many things—my dad, the dentist, Russ, my current situation of being broke and homeless, etc., but one of the main things was my loneliness. I had never been much of a ladies man and had only had one "real" girlfriend that only lasted six months or so and it had now been years since I had even talked to a girl. The longer I went without talking to any girls, the more difficult it seemed and I knew it was just a huge waste of time to even attempt to start a conversation because what would I say? Should I open by telling them I have no money and no home or should I save that for a surprise? There are millions of guys in L.A. that have both money and a home, so I didn't really stand a chance. It was very discouraging to come to terms with that. I felt like I was going to be alone forever because I was such a wreck. I tried not to think about it but there were girls and couples everywhere I turned to help remind me how alone I was.

Acting class was still all I really had going for me but even that got a lot more difficult because I was so self conscious. I was doing so good there for a while, but now all I could focus on was hearing myself say the lines and I could just feel everyone's eyes staring at me the whole time I did a scene. I stumbled through my lines and turned more red than I did when I first started. It just got to be too humiliating for me and I stopped going. I just told Gary that I needed to stop so I could catch up on paying him back because I was just digging myself into more debt with him. I really didn't want to stop going to class, but I was just too much of a wreck to make it worthwhile anymore.

Since I wasn't in class anymore and felt so embarrassed at how bad I was at acting the last few weeks, I didn't stay with Gary and Kate as much and stayed at my boss' more. I wasn't as comfortable there as I was with Gary, but I felt so bad staying at his house when I already owed him so much money. I still had the same kind of routine where I would waste time at a bookstore or coffee until it was late enough to just show up at my boss' and go to sleep. I was so paranoid of being in her way and it was kind of awkward hanging out with my boss on her couch anyway so I really didn't want to go over there until I needed to. She was a very nice person and I appreciated her letting me stay there, but it was just weird and I was too much of a social wreck to hang out with people anyway.

Because I needed to waste so much time before I went over to her house, I asked her if I could get any more hours at the zoo. Baseball season was over and I didn't have class anymore, so I needed to do something. She couldn't get me any more hours stocking churros or driving the tram but she did get me to work a couple of catering events held at the zoo. I never knew so many people had their parties at the zoo, but there had to have been at least two or three every week. They were all either fund raisers for the zoo or company parties and they were all held at night after the zoo closed so if I worked all day playing with churros and then worked at night at the parties, I would be getting around a fourteen hour day or so. I didn't mind working that much because what else did I have to do and working the parties was kind of fun. I started out by setting up the tables and the food stations and getting everything ready and then when the people showed up, I usually helped out with stocking the bar or whatever was needed. I was basically a runner the whole time and then I helped take everything down after the party was over. It was a pretty nice gig and the best part was I got to eat the left over food because they would make so much more than was needed for the party. Anytime there was a chance to eat I took it. That was the most difficult part of being broke was dealing with the hunger. I spent a lot of time with headaches because I was so hungry and when I did get to eat, I ate way to fast because I just wanted the headache to go away and to be able to get some energy as fast as I could. I still eat fast now and I never take for granted being able to eat whatever I want whenever I want.

As time went by at the zoo, I was getting to work more and more catering events and slowly started to do that more than slinging churros or driving the tram. I liked it a lot better and I got more hours so I was really starting to save up some money now and actually tinkered around with the idea of looking for an apartment. I still didn't have enough money to feel confident about it, but I at least was looking at how much rent would be at some places, so it was encouraging. The more I saved, the more promising it seemed that I was going to be able to find a place to live and then one day I decided to go apartment hunting. I spent the whole day looking at places and talking to managers and at the end of the day all my excitement was dead. Renting a decent apartment by myself was going to drain my savings and make me live paycheck to paycheck and that really wasn't going to work since my paychecks were never the same amount. I didn't want to get a place and three months in have to put all my stuff back in storage and live out of my truck again, so it seemed like I was looking at a few more months of homelessness at least.

I continued working as much as I could at the zoo and only bought the necessities-food and coffee, trying to save up as much money as I could, but it still seemed far fetched that I could afford an apartment by myself. The ones I could afford looked like they would be more trouble than anything and after spending the last seven or eight months without my own space or any of my things, I wanted a place where I could relax, not stress over what was going on outside and if my stuff was going to still be there when I got home after work.

I was about to just give in and take what I could afford because I didn't think I was in any position to be picky and that's when Arnold came back to visit, as he often did. I told him I was looking at places and he thought that was cool and then made me an offer. Since he was making good money on the soap and he was traveling back and forth from New York to L.A. a lot, he offered to split a two bedroom apartment with me so he would a have a place to stay when he came to visit and it would help me out because rent would be less expensive for me than a one bedroom apartment. I felt kind of weird accepting because I was so stubborn and didn't want anyone to help me, but it sounded like a good deal and I was really, really tired of not having anywhere to live. We went around and looked at two bedroom apartments and now that my half of the rent would be more manageable, the options looked a lot better. We ended up taking this place that was way beyond what I was expecting. It was a gated complex with a security guard out front to let you in and it had a huge pool, weight room, sauna, basketball court and BBQ area. It was fancy. The apartment itself was nicer than the townhouse we lived in before, I thought. It had an elevator that took us to our second floor pad and we walked in to an open living room with a bedroom on each side of it. Each bedroom had it's own bathroom right next to it and the kitchen overlooked the living room and was a pretty good sized kitchen for an apartment. Outside the living room was a little patio that overlooked a little side street so it was perfect. The bedrooms were good size and it was perfect that we each had our own bathroom. This place was the shit and I could not wait to get my stuff out of that tiny storage unit and let it all out in the apartment so it could breathe.

I think it was a week or so later that I was able to move in. Arnold went back to New York and I wish I could have been better at showing emotion because I don't think he knew how much I appreciated what he did. I know it helped him out as well with taxes and a place to stay and all, but it helped me out more than I could have put into words. I will be forever grateful for him helping me out.

I spent a total of ten months being homeless and I learned more in those ten months than I did in the previous twenty three years. What I used to think was important, became meaningless. What I used to think was stressful, was now a joke. What I used to think I *needed*, was now a waste of money. I learned how nice people can be and who my real friends were and I learned to never take a full stomach for granted. It certainly wasn't easy to be broke, hungry, and homeless on my own in a strange city, but it certainly could have been much worse. I didn't have to rat around in garbage's looking for recyclables, I never got beaten up and mugged, and I got to shower everyday. I'm also very lucky I had Gary and Kate and my boss Kayla that let me stay with them from time to time and I'm very lucky I got that job when I did. I wish I could repay them somehow and hopefully someday I will be able to.

10

I NOW HAD AN address and a mailbox but for some reason still didn't have a phone. I don't remember why I didn't get a phone hooked up in my new apartment, but for whatever reason I never did so I had to walk over to the 7-11 and use the pay phone there. My mom had sent me a phone card so I could call her no matter what so I used that and was still using my pager. Cell phones were just becoming the thing and I had gotten one, but I didn't know anything about them and was sold a crappy one with crappy service that would only allow me to get coverage if I was standing on a certain corner facing a certain direction at a certain time of day, so it was pretty much useless. And me, being my usual idiot self, signed a two year contract with the company and would have been charged hundreds of dollars if I would have broken the contract so I was stuck with it.

It didn't really matter though, I had a place to live and besides going to work, I was never going to leave my place anyway. It was so nice to sleep in my own bed, have food in the refrigerator, and sit on my own private toilet. All of my stuff that I had for years, looked brand new now and I felt like I was living like a king. I would come *home* after work, fix myself dinner in my kitchen and sit on the couch and eat while watching TV. I would then take a shower and get into my bed and go to sleep surrounded by walls and silence. It seemed I could not have been happier but the only thing missing was someone to share all of this with. Now that I had my own place and my mind wasn't in a constant state of stress, I had more time to realize how alone I was. I had not even talked to a girl in years and felt so alienated from that part of life that I just ached anytime I thought about it or even saw a girl. I wanted to be with someone so bad, but it seemed so out of reach. It had been way too long and I was way too shy to go up to a complete stranger and start a conversation and even though I felt immensely successful for getting back on my feet and getting an apartment, I'm sure the materialistic girls of L.A. wouldn't quite see it the same way as I did. I spent a lot of time laying in bed imagining what it would be like to have someone lying next to me and someone to talk to. It seemed like that was as close as I was ever going to get was just in my imagination though.

Even though having a place to live isn't that big of an accomplishment to most, it was to me and it gave me enough confidence to at least try to talk to girls. The only two public places I knew of where girls hung out were the bookstore and the coffee place. Those were the only places I ever went and no girls ever showed any interest in me there before, but now with my newborn confidence, I was sure I was going to be irresistible. I had a home for crying out loud! So I went to the coffee place and was writing like I always did. I was sitting inside by the window and every now and then looked out to watch the people sitting outside. I noticed this cute blonde girl sitting by herself out there. I went back to writing and when I looked up again, she was still there just looking around. I got caught staring at her and she smiled at me and I think I smiled back. I started to panic because I didn't know what to do. Should I go talk to her or should I just leave her alone and chalk this one up as a success because a girl smiled at me? I went back to writing and tried to concentrate but found myself looking up every two seconds to see if she was looking at me. She was still looking at me and so I thought this was it, I should get over my fear and just go say hi. My nerves got the best of me and I noticed all the people at the coffee place that would not only see me approach her but also hear me try to fumble my way through a conversation. I smiled at her and remained in my seat and tried to calm myself down before I would start the production of having everyone watch me try to be able to form the word "hi".

I was just about ready to do it. I was nervous but excited. I closed my notepad, put away my pen, gathered my stuff up and took one last look out at her. Right then a guy walked up to her and she stood up and kissed him. She then said something to him and they both turned and looked at me and started laughing. I avoided eye contact and when I looked up again they were gone. I sat there for a minute and couldn't believe how stupid I was to actually think her smile was inviting instead of condescending. I gathered up my stuff and walked out trying not to look at anyone because it felt like they all knew, although I'm sure they didn't. I got into my truck and headed back home where I wouldn't be able to embarrass myself anymore.

I stayed home a lot more after that and when I did go out to coffee or somewhere public, I just kept my head down and didn't even bother to try and trick myself into thinking I could get a girl to talk to me. It was just a lot easier that way. More frustrating and painful, but easier. I figured what if I did somehow start up a conversation with some young filly, how long would it last? I didn't have much going for me and I wasn't exactly the most talkative person in the world and every time I even talked to someone I knew, it seemed awkward and forced, so how uncomfortable would it be talking to a complete stranger? And I'm just talking about for me, not how it would be for the other person. So I pretty much went to work and then went home and that was my life for the next few months.

The zoo was going along fine and I started only working in the catering department and didn't have to drive the tram or cook churros much at all anymore. There started to be a lot more parties at the zoo and I became the catering managers' bitch. She was a very nice Puerta Rican lady and I started working for her all the time even when there wasn't any events. She had me take inventory of all the food and alcohol and organize all the catering stuff and when there was an event, I would still set it all up and break it all down. During the parties, I got to do a lot more now though. I would either be the guy who walks around with the appetizers or I would be the bartender. I didn't know how to make many drinks but most of those people wanted beer or wine anyway so it all worked out. Those were my favorite nights, I would be making overtime, tips, and got to hang out at a party at the zoo until one or two in the morning. Made it feel like I had a life and I was making pretty good money and I got to wear a bow tie.

One of the best parts of having my own place again was my mom and aunt got to come visit. I always looked forward to that because I missed them and it was always so much fun to show them around L.A. and go to the beach or just hang out. It made me feel normal again.

Most of the time we would go somewhere though. We went to San Diego and went to the animal park and the zoo one time, went to Disneyland another time and it was always great. The bad part was I always knew they had to go back home and that seemed to be all I could concentrate on. I would be so excited to go get them at the airport, but then it seemed like all I was doing was counting down and dreading the day when I would have to drop them off at the airport. I hated goodbyes and they were always tough for me. Their visits helped me out a lot though and those visits were some of the best times I have ever had.

Since I was making decent money and wasn't spending any of it on girlfriends or anything fun, I was able to save up and pay Gary back everything I owed him and started going back to class. I was still a self conscious, depressed wreck, but I missed it so much and now I didn't feel as guilty being there. When I went back, there were a lot of new people in the class and when it was time for me to go up and read a scene, it felt like the first time all over again. Nervous gas, dry mouth, and for some reason, the inability to read. I stumbled through every other word and just like the first time, I was all sweaty and my face was bright red. I was very aware of people watching me and I just wanted to tell everyone to turn around and not watch me while I read. It was weird, I loved being in the class and doing scenes but I hated being watched. I didn't want to entertain people, I just wanted to act out scenes and go through some of those emotions and play make believe. I was already wrong for acting because I was so shy and now I hated people watching me do scenes and having the attention on me, so I really shouldn't have been doing this. Everyone else wanted to be famous and have a big crowd to preform in front of and would even bring in their friends and family to watch them act. That was the last thing I wanted. I didn't want anyone I knew to see me act because I didn't want to get made fun of. I was reluctant do a lot in life because of the fear of being made fun of.

I was, and still am, more comfortable talking in front of people or being myself more in front of strangers than I am in front of people I know. It's complicated and doesn't make much sense. Here's an example: I can talk about art, acting, chicken wings or anything else I care about easier and less self consciously in front of strangers than in front of my friends or family. Even if there is a group of strangers and only one friend of family member is there, I shut down and am quiet. I just have this overwhelming fear of people who know me making fun of me. I don't know why and I should be over it by now, but I'm not. I'm just weird. I have accepted that.

So now things were back to normal for the most part. I had a place to live, a job, and was going to class again. Things were pretty boring there for a while and I was never so happy to have it so boring. But just as fast as I could say that, things changed again. Our one year lease was up on the apartment and they wanted to jack the price up so much I couldn't have afforded it. There was no real warning about it either and after all the little things that went wrong with the place in the last year, I marched into the leasing office and complained. I told the lady how they ruined some of my furniture when they used that extreme heat method to kill all the bugs in the apartment without telling me they were going to do it, how the gym and pool were constantly closed for the first month and a half I lived there, and how I was always hassled at the front gate even though I lived there and had a parking pass. Now they wanted to raise the rent hundreds of dollars without at least thirty days notice? She apologized for everything and told me I could move to another apartment in one of the other buildings and my rent would stay the same. Instead of my second floor apartment facing a little side street, it would be a first floor apartment facing a main street. I agreed because I didn't care about all that, I just cared about the price. So I had to move all of my stuff again for the fourth time in three years only this time I had to move it about a thousand feet to the next building. I moved it all by myself again so it took a while, but I eventually got it all done. I still wasn't too upset about having to do all that though because having a place to live is much better than not and I didn't want to take it for granted and be picky.

So my living situation was still good and my job was still good and my social life was about to get better it seemed. I still had not even talked to a girl in years, but somehow one of the catering girls seemed to talk to me more and more every event we did. It started out just work talk but as time went on she fell victim to my overwhelming charm and soon we were actually eating our left over catering food dinners together and walking each other to our cars after work. Her name was Sienna and she was a little blonde girl who kind of looked like Helen Hunt. I was just happy having a friend and someone to talk to and really wasn't ready to be in a relationship, as much as I wanted to be in one. I just knew I was too much of a wreck and I felt I needed to keep it safe and just be friends with her. She also had two kids and I certainly wasn't ready for all that. I pretty much never even had a girlfriend before, it would have been a bit too much to jump right in to being a family man. She was very nice and I really liked her but it was one of those times when I was over thinking everything and didn't want to mess things up by changing them. We stayed friends for a while and then one night we had to work a party and it was also my birthday. I was just planning on going home after work but when the party was over, she had a cake and a bottle of wine waiting for me. She wanted to know if we could go to my place and have the wine and I calmly said yes, even though inside I was freaking out. I was going to have a girl in my apartment! I couldn't believe it, I had finally made the big time! We went back and had some wine and talked and I felt so cool. Then the wine must have gotten to her because we kissed. Now I felt even cooler but it was more awkward than anything. I was so far out of my element and it wasn't safe anymore. My personal space that was protected by our friendship was now invaded and I was much too awkward and uncomfortable. I tried to play it off though and I think she felt weird about it too. We ended up just drinking more and talking the rest of the night and that was for the best. Of course, with talking comes criticism and it wasn't long before she was telling me what was wrong with me and how I need to let my shield down.

We tried to make it work the next few weeks but it never really clicked. I knew I was too weird for her and it was just easier to accept it. She was a good girl and I wish we could have made it work, but like a lot of things in my life, my mind got in the way.

I had now kissed one girl, one time, in the last three years. I was a huge slut. I thought it would help my confidence and get me going on the right track but all it did was make me realize how far away I was from being normal. I thought being with someone would help me not feel so alone but I felt even more alone and alienated around her and just about everyone else. Alone I didn't feel so self conscious and didn't feel the need to talk non stop about nothing just to fit in. I started to figure out that I didn't have to do the social activities and go hang out with people because I thought I needed to, I only needed to be able to feel comfortable doing those things and I didn't think I ever would.

Back at the zoo I was made an offer I couldn't refuse. There was a TV show on that was called The X Show, and it was kind of like a group talk show with all of these so called celebrities that would try and be funny and perverted. It was kind of like a less funny, less entertaining Man Show. Anyway, they rented a tram from the zoo to use for one of their shows and needed a driver and I was offered to do the job. I of course said yes and a couple of days later I showed up at Hollywood Studios and there was the tram waiting for me. They told me to drive it around all of these little studio streets and then back it into the set. I thought it was going to be no big deal, I had driven it quite a few times at the zoo but these streets were a lot more crowded and narrow. It took me quite a while to maneuver my way through all the people and parked cars but I eventually made it. Then it was time to back it into the set. I had never backed it in anywhere before and they wanted me to back it in and line it up on some tape, all the while not hitting the side walls that had about six inches on each side. Even though I had never done it before and wanted to tell them I couldn't, I pretended I had been there before and acted like I was an expert. Somehow I nailed it. Exactly on the tape and I didn't hit anything. I was so proud of myself.

I spent the next twelve hours sitting in the drivers seat and every scene change or commercial break, I would move the tram up or back about twenty feet so it looked like it was somewhere else. I watched the show the following week when it aired and I saw myself for about 2.7 seconds but the tram sure did look good.

Although my new found celebrity status was taking the zoo by storm, it still didn't help with the ladies. I couldn't even talk to any of them in a work situation without getting all nervous and shutting down. I didn't know what else I needed to do, I mean I had a lot to offer: I was now a major television star, I had an apartment, and I had unlimited access to free churros. If all that couldn't give me the confidence I needed, what would?

Then one day Arnold called me and told me he had this friend from Nashville that was coming to L.A. for a few days and wanted to know if I would want to hang out with her. I said why not and soon after she called me. We talked for a long time on the phone which was weird for me since I wasn't much of a talker, and she told me she would be in town the next week and we should go out. After I hung up, I was pretty excited. The conversation went well and it wasn't awkward at all and I was looking forward to going out with her.

When she showed up we decided to meet at some Mexican restaurant and that's where I made my first mistake. I offered to go pick her up at her hotel but she kept saying that she would take a cab. I kept offering and she kept saying no and after the fourth time, I just agreed to meet her there. She would later tell me how wrong I was for letting her take a cab.

When we first met at the restaurant, I thought she was really cute and after our good conversation on the phone, I thought I might stand a chance. We had a few drinks and then had dinner and it was going pretty good for the most part but it seemed like she wanted to know a lot more about Arnold than anything. She kept asking how things were going with him and his girlfriend, what he was like growing up and it ended up feeling like I was their matchmaker more than anything. The few times she asked me about me, it was followed by her telling me what was wrong with me and how I should change. That kind of put a damper on the evening. After dinner we went back to my place where she continued to be my therapist and counselor, telling me I had this giant shield up protecting me all the time and wouldn't let anyone in or even close to me. By the end of the evening, I felt like everything was wrong with me and Arnold was perfect.

She went back to Nashville a few days later and I never heard from her again. I guess I should have picked her up at her hotel.

Answering questions about Arnold seemed to be a common theme for me. He was my best friend and everything but it was tough always being the other guy. He was the tall, good looking one that could get any girl he wanted and I was just his short, quiet friend. Most of the time when we went out together to a bar or something, the girls would only talk to me to get to him. I got used to feeling like the third wheel most of the time and usually ended up drinking too much and that was my night out. Most of my memories from going out to bars or clubs in L.A. with Arnold and our friends consist of me standing there drinking while they would talk to girls. I was jealous.

Acting class was going good and I was getting better at not being so self conscious. I was still nervous every time I was up there but I figured out that if I wasn't nervous, something was wrong. It's boring watching someone who isn't risking some sort of embarrassment. I used to think acting was for the people who were comfortable in front of people and for people who liked the attention, but I was beginning to find out how wrong I was. All of the shy people in class were really good and you kind of got sucked in while watching them do their scenes and all the "performers" who were up there making acting faces were boring. I started figuring out that the actors who were wrapped up in what they were doing and how their reactions looked, were headed in the wrong direction. Too many people were concerned about how *they* were acting.

One night I was doing a scene and all of a sudden it all clicked for me and I realized what it was all about. I had been so concerned about what *I* was doing this whole time that I didn't even notice what the other actor was doing. We did the scene again and this time all I did was focus on the other person and try to shock them so much that they would forget their lines. It worked and it was so much more fun than the way I had been doing it before when all I did was focus on how I said my lines. The next few times, that's all I did was try to mess the other actor up and it was great. I started to see how fun it was to try and get the other actor to react the way I wanted them to just by looking in their eyes and trying to see what they were thinking. Just doing that alone got rid of my self consciousness because you can't concentrate on two things at once, so I tried to concentrate on at least their eyes instead of me.

As time went on I got more and more addicted to trying to figure out what was going on in the other actors head and trying to get them to react a certain way and it was paying off because I was getting complimented a lot on how good I was getting. They might have just been saying that to be nice, but I didn't care, I felt better doing the scenes now and that's all that mattered to me. I was really looking forward to class nights now and couldn't get enough. It wasn't even so much the scenes or the "acting" part, it was the figuring people out that fascinated me.

I was starting to understand the difference between the good actors and everyone else now. I was watching some movie with Al Pacino in it and I noticed how he was always staring intently on the other actor and I could just see him looking for that one little reaction to jump on. All he was doing was reading the other person and adjusting his own actions on the other persons reactions to get them to do what he wanted.

The best example I ever heard about what acting is really all about is a child in a toy store who wants a certain toy. The kid wants his mom to buy him that toy and that's all that matters. He asks for the toy and she says no. He then adjusts and sees if pouting will work. After reading his mom and figuring out that pouting isn't working, he adjusts and starts being nice. If that doesn't work, he starts crying. If that doesn't work, he throws a temper tantrum or runs away and hides. He does whatever it takes for him to get that toy and isn't self conscious about how he looks or how he's acting. That's what good actors do. They want the other actor to react in a certain way and will do whatever mind games it takes to get them to do it. Once I figured that out, that's all I tried to do and it was a whole new world for me. I was still nervous beforehand, but once the first word was spoken in the scene I couldn't concentrate on the nerves anymore because I was just listening to the other actor. It was a lot harder than it seemed and I wasn't very good at it, but it sure was a lot more fun to do a scene and I wanted to get better.

Even though I was really motivated to get better at acting, I still wasn't motivated to become an actor. It sounds weird because what's the point of going through class and trying to get better at something if you're not going to try to do it for a living, but I wasn't ever really all that concerned with that. I loved to act, but I hated the acting business, the scene, and the majority of people in it. Everything about it was fake, pretentious, and self glorifying and I really wanted no part of it. Not that I had a lot of experience with auditioning or anything, but the few times I did, it just sucked. Most of the people were self absorbed assholes who thought they were genius' and were acting like they were making a ground breaking cure for cancer instead of a commercial for antacids. I knew I wouldn't be able to communicate and work with these type of people who took themselves way too seriously.

Of course I'm sure there are very good, talented people out there, but they seem few and far between and the road to get to them isn't worth it in my opinion. It wasn't just about who you knew, it was about who you blew and was all an ego trip. I wasn't about to be fake and kiss someones ass just to get a chance to be on TV, I had been through too much to pretend to be something I'm not.

At the beginning of each class we would have to go around and tell everyone what auditions or jobs we got the last week and just about everyone had at least one every week. Every time it came to me though, I had nothing and everyone looked at me like I was from another planet because I had not even attempted to get an agent or anything. I actually did try to get an agent long before though and going through that process made me not want an agent. They were all douche bags with their over the top enthusiasm and two hundred dollar haircuts and I just didn't want to have to talk to them on a regular basis.

I never said anything in class about it though, I just said I wasn't ready for all that yet, which was mostly true. I was never going to be ready. I honestly just liked being in class. That was it for me and I was happy with it. I liked doing a few different scenes every time and just trying to get better without all the bullshit. I always thought that if there was someway to get paid to go to class, it would be perfect. Just go up and do some scenes with the people there and no one else. I didn't want an audience, cameras, or any of that, I just wanted to act. If I threw in all that other stuff and took it seriously, I would have hated it. This was a hobby for me and that's all. Well, it was therapy for me as well.

There are a lot of reasons people want to become actors. Very few do it for the artistic reasons: to tell a story, to teach humans about humans, to say something they need to say, or to tell the truth no matter how difficult it may be to hear. Some want to become actors to build their egos back up and get the attention they so desperately think they need. And most want to become actors because they are fascinated with celebrities and that lifestyle. They have looked up to movie stars since they were little and want people to look up to them as well. They are ordinary people who want to be fascinating for no other reason than to be fascinating because they really don't have anything original about them. It's not about expressing their deep down emotional truths with them, it's about expressing their fetish for fame, fashion, and the lifestyle that goes along with it. Most celebrities are not very good actors, they are just good celebrities, and the people that want to become actors should realize that. There are a million people that want to become famous and they are all going about things the same way, going to the same classes, talking about the same people, and listening to the same people and their advice. Instead, watch where everyone else is going and then go the other way and be seen. Standing out is rare and standing out because you are more than an enthusiastic 'yes man' with a purchased identity is even more rare and more advantageous. I wish there were more people who wanted to be known for what they could do with their own original talent, not just known for what shows they have been on, who they are dating, and where they shop.

I'm not done bitching about these people yet. It's just these people are so naive and it's television and film that is taking the worst of it. As much as I like acting, I really don't like movies. The originality of them is gone and I find the majority of them so boring because of it. They are all made with the same dramatic and comedic timing which makes it hard to get into and too predictable. I can't be shocked or convinced of something when there is still a half hour left in the movie, I know it's just going to change. It just all seems like everyone is copying everyone else. The predictability, the cliches, and the special effects are all the same and I find myself losing interest and looking around the room more than at the screen. A lot of that has to do with my short attention span, but still, someone please do something original with actors who want to be good, not just ones who want to be on the cover of a magazine.

I have never done anything more than a few auditions and a class, I don't know anything and don't claim to be an expert, these are just my opinions, and I know that criticizing is the easiest thing in the world to do and I shouldn't criticize unless I can do better. We only criticize what we don't understand and I don't understand how these people can be so impressionable and are unable to think for themselves.

That being said, I will continue to vent. A lot of people who want to become actors, or more specifically, famous, automatically get into an acting class of some sort. There are hundreds of them in L.A. and it's pretty overwhelming to have to pick one or "get accepted" to one. I was lucky and found one that had more positives than negatives to me. I looked at a few others later on and could not believe that so many people fall for this shit. There were so many classes out there that base their whole existence on taking advantage of the young and not so young naive wannabe actors who were ready to listen and believe any and all advice that was given to them, no matter where it came from.

As I have said before, you can only learn to do something by doing it. If you want to learn how to play the piano, you actually play the piano, you don't spend three months doing finger exercises and pretending to play the piano. If you want to learn to act, you do acting scenes, not speech exercises or pretending you're an animal. That's all I saw out of the majority of those classes was a whole lot of "self observing exercises" that only made people focus on themselves and what they were doing and really had nothing to do with good acting. In doing so, it only prolonged the entire process and it was months before any of them even got to do a real scene and got to "start" acting. This of course was job security for the teachers because the students had to be there for a long time without really doing anything productive. It reminded me of college and my mini blind installing revelation. Wasting a whole lot of time going through steps that are completely unnecessary only to find out there is a much more productive way. If people wouldn't automatically listen and believe what everyone told them they "needed" to do and just thought for themselves and did what they themselves thought was needed, there would be a lot more diverse personalities out there, resulting in a lot more original actors.

And it boggles my little tiny brain that some of these classes had to "accept" who would be their students. The second I heard that, I turned around and ran away. If you have to be accepted and good enough to be able to pay them to learn, then all they are doing is auditioning you so they can take credit for you later on when you make it. The Actors Studio used to do that and I never understood that. I have heard that James Deans audition to get into the Actors Studio was the best work he ever did in his whole career. If that was his best, before he even got into the class, then how can they take credit for teaching him and doesn't that kind of sound like the class actually made him worse? They probably overcomplicated everything for him and got him into his head.

The Actors Studio was great though for it's time because all the big names came from there, but it started this whole trend of classes advertising all of the famous people that studied with them and that sucked a lot of people in. I don't know if they realized that just because so and so went there, that's not why they made it. James Dean was going to make it whether he went to the Actors Studio or not. Just because you are in the same class as Brad Pitt once was, doesn't mean you will learn how to be like Brad Pitt. (Who in my opinion, isn't a very good actor anyway, but he is a good celebrity.)

The other trend it started was needing to be good enough to get into the class so you could be taught to take their advice, the same advice they are giving everyone else. How can you be original if you are learning from the same point of view that everyone else is? I know a lot of them would give advice like how to take a speech class to be able to speak clearer. So now you have twenty people all rushing to take a speech class so they can learn how to speak "better" even though all it does is take time and energy away from actually getting better at acting. You can always tell who has taken the speech classes too, it all sounds so unnatural and over enunciated. Marlon Brando never needed to take a speech class. He did all right.

I also never understood why some of these classes wanted you to watch yourself on tape after you did a scene. If you need to watch yourself in order to improve, you are only improving your self consciousness and will only be focusing on what your reactions look like. That's not good acting because it's not very interesting for us to watch you being all wrapped up in thinking about having a bigger reaction. We want to see honest reactions that the actor didn't even see coming, not a bunch of thought out emotions and exaggerated looks. We are fascinated by watching a crazy man on the street tying his shoe because no one knows what he is going to do next, not even him.

If you are thinking about anything other than how you want the other actor to react in a scene, you're not acting very well and it shows. Improve by watching the other actor, not yourself. I know a lot of these methods are because that's what the teacher wants you to do, and that's the problem. Everyone just automatically assumes they know nothing and the teacher knows the secret. If they knew the secret, they wouldn't be teachers.

In the class I was in, I didn't take it too seriously and treated it like I was a reading a book. I took the parts from it I needed or wanted and forgot the rest. I wasn't impressionable enough to just sit there and take in everything and adopt a whole new style of thinking, I was stubborn and wanted to do what I wanted to do, the way I thought I needed to do it. I never was, and still am not, a very good student.

That class was great and perfect for me though because we didn't do all of those unnecessary exercises, all we did was scenes from movies and plays. It was just practicing what you would be doing. That's it. No practicing crying, no practicing laughing, no remembering how you felt when you lost your pet rock when you were five. We only did scenes and focused on getting the other person to react the way we wanted. It wasn't about how *you* acted, it was about how you got the other person to act. I still think that is the only way to go. There is a lot more that goes into it later on, but if you can just do that, you are miles ahead of everyone else. All that other stuff gets actors in their head and makes them only care about how they are reacting, resulting in a lot of blank looking eyes and what I call "confused acting", where no matter what is going on in the scene or what it's about, the actor acts confused and like he is trying to figure out something.

All I'm saying is be very specific to what you want to do and do it the way you want to do it. No one knows what you want and need more than you, so don't think you need other people to tell you what that is. Think for yourself and take responsibility for yourself. Be original.

All right, now that I got that out of my system, I can move on.

Class was good, work was good, home was good, social life wasn't so good. For the next few months, that was my life. Arnold was coming back to visit a lot more with his girlfriend, Christy, and it wasn't much longer before his contract was up on the soap, so he was planning on moving back with her. I think the plan was for all of us to live together and that was fine by me, I was ready to have some liveliness in the apartment and some friends. Since Christy hated living in New York and I got along with her really well, the decision was made to have her move back to L.A. and in with me a few months before Arnold moved back. Sounded good and it was good at first. I now had a friend, she was happier in L.A. and everything was gonna be peachy once Arnold moved back.

Then the drama started. I don't remember what started it, but all of a sudden me and her couldn't stand each other. We used to be really good friends and went and did stuff together and then it all stopped. We constantly argued and everything I said was taken the wrong way and was completely blown out of proportion. It wasn't just her fault, I was still a lonely wreck and I'm sure my bitterness came through more than it should have, but it got kind of ridiculous. I remember this one time I was going to go meet some girl out at a bar and I asked Christy if she wanted to meet us there and have some drinks. Even though this girl I was meeting was just a friend of mine, I still thought it would be too awkward for just the two of us to hang out so I was hoping Christy would go so it would make it a little more comfortable. She said yes and she would for sure be there. She ended up not showing up and when I went back home, I knocked on her bedroom door, heard her say something and opened the door and asked why she didn't show up. She said she didn't feel like it and the way she said it kind of irritated me and I told her how I wish she could have just called me and told me she wasn't coming so I wasn't stuck there all night waiting. I left and went to my room and from that night forward, we never got along again and she accused me of breaking into her room and trying to kill her. When I talked to Arnold about it, he told me she was quite the drama queen and he didn't know if he could deal with her anymore. They soon broke up, she moved out, and I was back to living alone, but alone was better than having a roommate accusing me of trying to kill them by opening their door.

My guess is she was trying to make me the bad guy so Arnold and I wouldn't be friends anymore and she could live with only him. I guess she was kind of possessive from what he has told me. She used to get all jealous anytime he would want to see his mom and that ended up being a big reason why they broke up.

I had not had very good luck with roommates and it wasn't too long before Arnold was going to move back in. I was really hoping he wouldn't end up hating me too, like all my other roomies ended up doing.

11

THREE YEARS, SOME hunger, some homelessness, and a soap opera later, Arnold and I were roommates again. It was very exciting to have a real friend again and it was fun to have him move all of his stuff in and redo the apartment. He had good stuff and it made the apartment feel like it was lived in, not just rented out. I was happy to have him back and be my roommate again. Although we only lived together for a few months before, he was the only person I liked living with. I always fought with all my other roommates and a lot of that had to do with me being stubborn and not wanting to listen to them tell me what was wrong with me. It also had to do with them not understanding that I was a loner and needed my alone time. I think Arnold understood that and didn't push it and just let me be.

Just about everything was going pretty good for the first time in a long time. I had a good roommate and friend, a good job, class was going good and thanks to an earthquake, I made some more friends. It happened during a weekend when Arnold was out of town. We had made friends with a girl (actually Arnold did and I just got to talk to her every once in awhile) who lived across the hall from us. She was a very good looking blonde girl named Amy who lived alone and who was always outside of her apartment smoking. Anyway, when Arnold was away, she would talk to me and I was over at her place eating some of her food when all of a sudden their was a loud boom and the walls started shaking. She freaked out and I grabbed her and we went outside. I didn't know what we were supposed to do during an earthquake, but I figured outside would be better than being inside a first story apartment with three more stories above us. I had been through a few earthquakes by now, they were pretty common in L.A. and this one wasn't a big deal, but Amy had never been in one before so she was too freaked out to go back in her place for a while and while we were outside, a few of the neighbors were still outside as well. One guy was covered in tattoos and had a Mohawk and his earlobes were all stretched out. He was freaked out too but that was mainly paranoia from smoking pot all day. Another guy was just chubby. He was from New York and had just moved there and he had never even heard of an earthquake before, so he was all pale and quiet. We started talking to them and before I knew it, we were all sitting outside together drinking beer. It turned out to be a really fun night and we all started hanging out together afterward.

The tattoo guys name was Edward and he was trying to be an architect. He was intimidating looking but was a very nice guy and couldn't decide if he wanted to be gay or not. The New Yorker was named Seth and he had moved to L.A. to be a stand up comedian. I guess that's what he did in New York but came to L.A. so there would be a better chance of getting on a sit com or something. He was a very nice guy as well and he was sure he didn't want to be gay.

Since we all lived on the same floor and our front doors were within a hundred feet of each other, it became like a sit com where we would all just go and either just walk into each others place or at least hang out in someones apartment. It was really cool and for the first time ever, I felt like I had friends. Amy was a really good painter and I talked to her about that a lot, Edward was a wreck but had a sense of humor about it and he was always somebody that was ready to go and do anything at anytime, Seth was the mature one that you could talk to about anything, and of course Arnold was like family.

It was a nice change to have people to talk to all the time and I had something to look forward to when I came home after work now. We really didn't ever go anywhere together, we all were just kind of happy sitting at home and drinking original concoctions from our wide variety of alcohol bottles I had gotten on discount. Ok, I had taken them from the zoo. Since I was in charge of doing all the inventory for the food and alcohol in the catering department, I had unlimited access to it all and had my own golf cart and I was told to load up and throw away any alcohol that hadn't been used in the last few events. I started loading up all the bottles that we never used into the back of my golf cart and was headed across the street to the big dumpster when I passed my truck in the parking lot. I thought why should we waste all of this alcohol when I could take it all home and keep the party going out on our patio?

Some of those bottles weren't even opened yet and the ones that were, only had a shot or two missing out of them, so why dump it all out? I threw the box of booze in my truck and no one knew. As time went on and our livers started absorbing more and more alcohol, the "bad" alcohol that I was supposed to be throwing away seemed to increase for "inventory reasons". Wink, wink.

We now had enough alcohol in our apartment to fully stock an Irish bar on St. Patrick's Day and our patio parties kept going. It was fun, but the more I drank, the more my depression sank in. It was great having friends and all, but I still wanted to be able to at least talk to a girl. I really liked Amy but I could tell she didn't want anything to do with me and I figured it would be better to just be friends anyway since we were all getting along so good and I didn't want to ruin that. I tried not to let my loneliness and depression show too much, but it got really tough when Arnold would bring girls home. I was happy for him and wanted him to do whatever he wanted, but it was really tough for me to be the odd man out. He could get any girl he wanted and I had only kissed one girl, one time, in the last four years. Being out in the living room while he and a girl were talking or watching a movie together was like eating steak and lobster in front of a starving man. I wasn't mad at him at all, but I was jealous. I wanted to be like that and be comfortable around someone and have a girl cuddle up to me.

The more times that happened, the more I felt I needed to get out of their way, so I usually just went to my room and watched TV or painted. When we would all hang out together and drink, I would be fine up until I hit a point, then all I could think about was how much it hurt to be so alone. I would get really self conscious and feel like people would start making fun of me or start criticizing me so I would just make some excuse and go to my room. It was so tough to be so weird. I hated sitting in my room alone hearing people out there having fun and being normal, but I also didn't want to go out there and be self conscious and have to defend myself on why I was being so quiet. I just wanted to be a normal twenty three year old who could be comfortable around people.

I started hiding in my room a lot more and I never realized how that came across. Arnold thought I was mad at him or something and everyone else thought I was weird, which I was. I wasn't mad at Arnold at all, I was just so wrapped up in my own little head and it was so hard to see him with all of these girls, that I just thought it would be better if I kept to myself. I knew I wasn't much fun and I didn't want to be a downer, so I just let him be. I was just jealous of him and his life and it was hard for me to be around because I knew how far away I was from that.

I don't think anyone realized, not even me, how hard it was for me to be so lonely. I had been through a lot of mentally draining experiences in my life but the toughest was to be so alienated from a social life or love life. I thought having friends would help me, but once I had some, all it did was show me how far away I was from being normal and made me feel more alone. I thought all I needed was a girlfriend and that would fix everything, but I was starting to figure out that I only needed to be comfortable around myself before I could be comfortable around anyone else. That was discouraging because that seemed impossible right now.

As time went on, I had my good days and my bad days. Sometimes I would be social and hang out on the patio with everyone and have a good time. My bad days I spent in my room listening to everyone through the walls wishing I could fit in but knowing better.

I really liked Amy and was kind of hoping I could straighten myself up enough to get her to see I wasn't a complete freak, but before I knew it, her and Arnold were getting friendly. That progressed and soon he was staying over at her place all night. From then on, she wouldn't even talk to me unless it was to ask me where Arnold was and the only time I ever saw her was when she came over to see Arnold. I don't blame her for not wanting to be around me, I was a wreck and my unpredictable moods didn't help. I realize that now.

I don't blame them for getting together, it was only a matter of time and it made them both happy, but things weren't the same after they hooked up. Edward and Seth didn't hang out as much, partly because of me and partly because it now seemed like Arnold and Amy were more of an item than just friends and no one really wants to hang around a couple when they don't have anyone themselves, and I stayed in my room even more because I selfishly didn't want to be in the way, so it just wasn't as much fun as it was there for a while.

It also wasn't as much fun in class lately so I made the decision to stop going to class for a while. I loved it but I just needed a break from it and I was actually getting too depressed to do it. I only had one emotion:

sad, and it was tough to focus on what I was supposed to be doing. I was planning on going back, I just needed a little time away from it so I could maybe focus on becoming a sane person.

Somehow I was again offered a little bit of a higher position at the zoo. They were opening a coffee shop that sold Starbucks coffee. It wasn't a Starbucks though! I got that imbedded in my brain the first day. They only needed to tell me that once but I guess a thousand times was good too. Anyway, I was offered to be the manager of the place. I had no idea what that was going to involve, but I said I would do it. I would only have do that now, no churros, no tram, no catering events unless I really wanted to, and I would get one weekend day off, so it sounded perfect. We had a few weeks to set the entire place up and it was weird because people would come up to me and ask how things should be done. I felt very out of place making decisions on all of this, but just pretended like I knew what I was doing.

Then they brought in a Starbucks guy to teach us all about their coffee. It was much more involved than I had expected, but by the end of it, I knew everything there was to know about Starbucks and how to brew their coffee. It was a lot like a wine tasting class too. We had to try all the different brews and see the differences. They all pretty much tasted the same to me but I pretended I could tell the difference.

We were all set to open in a few days and I was a little nervous about being in charge. I was nervous about my mind getting the best of me and me not being able to handle it. When I was at work, I could function and keep my mind busy enough to not let the depression take over, but I didn't know how long I could keep doing that.

One morning I was woken up by the phone ringing and the machine picked up. It was one of our friends, Jacob, and he was saying something about planes and buildings or something, I couldn't really hear because the machine was in the other room and I was just waking up and I'm even more retarded when I'm trying to wake up, so I couldn't comprehend it anyway. A few minutes later Amy came over and asked us if we saw what was going on. We had been asleep, so we had no clue. She told us to turn the news on and we saw the Towers burning. We sat there and watched as the first tower collapsed. Arnold was pretty freaked out since he lived there and had just moved back. I didn't know what to think, I didn't know New York and thought that it was just a plane that crashed into it accidentally. Then when I saw the second tower get hit, I started freaking out. Then I heard about the building in Washington got hit. I freaked out some more. It was an eerie feeling and I was thousands of miles away, I couldn't imagine what it must have been like for the people that were there. We all watched the news and didn't say much, we just stared at the TV. It was more confusing than anything for me. I had never paid attention to all the political news and current world events, so I didn't know why all of this was happening. I continued to watch the news until it was time for me to get ready to go to work. I figured I still had to go to work even though I didn't see the point. Right before I left the house, I saw the second tower go down and sat back down and watched some more. I figured this would be a pretty good excuse for me being a few minutes late if there ever was one. I watched for a while and then headed off to the zoo which seemed really weird to me. The country was being attacked by terrorists, all government and state buildings were closed, just about the whole city of L.A. shut down, but I had to go to work and make coffee at the zoo.

I was hoping that once I got to work, they would just send us home, but nope, we had to be there to open up the coffee place for the two people that went to the zoo that day, neither of which wanted any coffee. I ended up drinking about a gallon and a half of coffee that day and got all wired and watched the news. It was great, I couldn't sit still and was all paranoid that L.A. was going to get hit next. Finally at around three, they told us we could go home.

The drive home never felt so weird. The L.A. freeways didn't have more than three cars on them and the cars on the surface streets were in no hurry, both were something I had never seen before. When I got home, all the neighbors were outside drinking and Seth looked exhausted. New York was his hometown and he had only moved away a few months before and he hadn't heard from any of his family or friends. Everyone was in a pretty somber mood, but he really looked beat down.

The next few days I still had to go to work even though everything else was shut down. There was a total of maybe eight people that visited the zoo in three days and that made my job even more boring. I was used to doing the heavy lifting and bouncing around to all the different spots in the zoo, not standing around in one spot all day, and now that there weren't any people going to the zoo, I really had nothing to do. I really thought it was stupid that we had to be there and I think I started getting an attitude about it. Why were we there to serve the public when there was no public? Everyone was afraid that L.A. would be attacked next, so most people wanted to be home. I know I did. If I was going to die, I didn't want to be at work when it happened.

I took a couple of sick days after that and when I went back, the zoo was still a ghost town. They decided to close the coffee place for a while and since everyone canceled their parties at the zoo as well, I couldn't even work any catering events. It looked like I was going to get my wish and have some time off.

Some time turned into a long time and soon they told me I could come in every once in a while, but there probably wouldn't be much work until the spring. I now had to look for a new job. Be careful what you wish for.

I spent two years working at the zoo and it is still one of my favorite jobs I've ever had. As much as I liked it there, I didn't fight very hard to stay and I wish that I would have. I had a good thing going but let my mind and the overwhelming depression control too much, like my decision making and drive. I really didn't care that I was getting laid off and didn't have the energy to fight it because of the depression. I didn't care about much anymore and that was what was making my decisions for me. Whatever was easiest, that's all that mattered. It was just easier to hide in my room and not deal with other people and see how life was supposed to be lived. It was just easier to to quit class than to keep going and risk any embarrassment, and it was easier to just be laid off than to argue and fight for a job I deserved. When I thought about how difficult it might be to find a new job, I actually considered just giving up and being homeless again just because it was easier than going through the job interview process and struggling to pay rent.

For the next few months, it was back to being broke and panicking. It was hard to find a job before, but now it was pretty much impossible. I didn't know what I was going to do and was getting kind of sick of that being my life's theme. I went back home for Thanksgiving and tried to figure it out. Being home and around my mom made me feel better and dulled the depression enough where I could look ahead and see some hope. While I was there, my uncle said I could come back to Reno and work for Desiderio again even for a month or two and save up some money if I wanted to do. It sounded good, but I wasn't sure if I wanted to go through moving again even if it was just a few things and I wasn't sure Desiderio wouldn't lay me off two weeks after I got there. I told him I would think about it and then went back to L.A.

I thought about it a lot the next few days and it sounded better and better. I looked around and saw my life in L.A. going nowhere and it would be a while before it turned around because the whole city was freaked out over the terrorists, so nothing was going to get going anytime soon. I loved going to class but that was just a hobby and if I was never going to pursue it, then it just seemed like a dead end. My little group of friends didn't hang out much and Arnold was always hanging around Amy and I was tired of being the third wheel. I needed a break from it all and this was the perfect opportunity. I loved L.A. and didn't want to move away from it, but I just needed to get my money and my mind back to normal. I called my mom and told her I was going to come back for Christmas and I would stay and work for a while. Of course that made her happy, but it was tough for me to accept that I was a failure and had to go to another city just to find a job.

I went back and started working again and lived at my moms. It was really nice to be around her and the dogs and to have it so much more mellow that it had been in awhile. The job was the same as it was years before only now I got to do more. I didn't really concentrate on the job though, I just went through the motions and tried to think about how I would be able to save up enough money and go back to L.A. soon.

It had been a month or so I think and the job was going good and I was saving some money and learning a lot more than I did during my first run at Desiderio. I was a lot harder of a worker now than I was then, thanks to the zoo, and Neal who still worked there was starting his own contractor business and told me I could work with him on the side if I decided to move back. He would pay me more than double what I was making there and it would be all cash. I had a lot of deciding to do now.

I went back and forth on the pros and cons of moving back to Reno and as much as I loved L.A., things were going nice and smooth in Reno and it just made more sense at the time. I told my mom I decided to move back and she was very happy. I told Arnold and he was kind of bummed I think. I told my uncle and he was happy and offered me his big truck to take back down to L.A. to get my stuff. Those were all the people I told and the only people it affected.

I drove to L.A. by myself and was going to spend a week or so and get all my stuff packed and loaded up. When I got there and started the whole moving process again, it was a lot more difficult than I was hoping it would be. I really, really didn't want to move but I had to do what I had to do. I couldn't keep struggling to pay the bills and to remain sane. I knew Reno would be for the best right now and in the back of my mind I knew I was going to be able to come back to L.A. before too long. That was the plan at least.

After a week of packing and stacking, I was ready to load up the truck and drive back to Reno in the morning. It made me sad to know that this wouldn't be my home anymore and I got in the truck and took one last drive around L.A. to reflect. I pulled over by the first place we lived in when I first moved there and remembered how excited I was when I pulled up and saw Arnold out there and how excited I was about everything then. It was all so new and I had so much hope and energy. I thought about all the good and not so good times I had while I lived there. All the good times with Arnold, Scott, and Jacob. All the not so good times of coming back home defeated by job interviews, dead truck batteries, and a few job terminations. I thought about how much of a mess I left the place when I had to leave and how scared I was that I had nowhere to go when I closed that door for the last time.

As I pulled the truck out onto the street, I passed the spot I had parked in when I slept in my truck that first night of homelessness. It seemed so long ago and I seemed like a such a different person then, yet I wasn't too far away from ending up in that position again.

I drove by the coffee place I spent hours and hours in and thought about how I was really going to miss just sitting there writing and people watching. That by far was my favorite activity for the last four years. And for some reason, I still remembered that girl and her boyfriend that laughed at me and how stupid I felt. It wasn't that big of a deal, I don't know why I still thought about it.

I went by the bookstore and the zoo and remembered how much I learned from both of those places and how both of them helped me so much when I was struggling. I was really going to miss the zoo.

Next I headed over to Santa Monica and drove by the park I slept in and drove around the streets that I used to walk around for hours on end. I spent so much time just walking with no destination in mind, but I guess in some way, I was always at least moving forward.

I then went and pulled into the parking lot of where my class was and just sat there in my truck and thought about how much that place had changed me. I couldn't help but think what could have happened if I would have been in a different state of mind when I was going to class. Would I have been better at it and actually tried to pursue a career in acting if I hadn't been such a head case and wouldn't have been struggling just to keep myself fed? Everyone in class always told me I should have pursued it because they thought I was good enough to make it. What if they were right? What if I would have been a little more stable and just had an ounce of confidence, would that have made a difference? What if that would have changed my whole perspective on everything? I guess it didn't matter anymore, I couldn't live my life thinking about all the 'what if's' and had to accept all the decisions I had made, no matter how bad they seemed.

It was time to stop over thinking everything and time to go back and load up the truck and get ready to drive back to Reno in the morning.

The next morning I woke up early, took one last look around the apartment, got a little teary eyed, and went to see if Arnold was awake to say goodbye. He wasn't in his room which meant he was over at Amy's, so I grabbed the last bag of my stuff and headed to the truck. I didn't knock on Amy's door, I didn't want to disturb them so early in the morning. I started up the truck, waved to the security guard as he opened the gate for me and headed back to Reno.

12

I DID A LOT of thinking on my nine hour drive back to Reno and I finally accepted that I was a failure and I needed to change that. I still did not know what I wanted to do with my life, but I didn't want to keep screwing it up like I had been. I planned on going back to work for Desiderio during the day and working with Neal for a few hours after that and on the weekends. I would keep my mouth shut, do what I was told, and work as hard as I possibly could and save up as much money as I could. I would then move back to L.A. and start over and not let my mind ruin everything again.

After working two jobs and living at my moms for a few months, I was able to save some money and some sanity. I didn't really like the type of work I was doing, but I learned to not take a job so personally and to just shut up, do the job as best as I can, and get my paycheck. I never thought about work once I left the place and found it was much better that way. I was only there to get a paycheck, I didn't want to become a boss, I didn't want change things there, and I didn't get wrapped up in all of the complaining about how things were run. I wanted to do what my job was as best as I possibly could do it and get my paycheck. That was all. I wanted to distance my work life from my personal life as much as possible and never have them affect each other again.

After a few months I had enough money that I could move back to L.A. but now I had my doubts. Things were going along nice and boring in Reno and it was nice. And I had been working hard at two jobs for the last few months and I didn't want to lose it all again if things didn't work out in L.A. I kept trying to decide if I was ready to move or not but kept putting it off. Anytime I would say anything about it at work, my uncle and Neal would tell me how stupid I was for wanting to go back. They didn't understand how much I liked it there and how just because things didn't go so well before, doesn't mean it would have always been like that. I always argued with them, but the more they talked, the more I let it sink in. I figured I would just keep a good thing going and decide later.

I was finally starting to see light at the end of the depression tunnel. I was still so lonely it hurt, but overall, I was able to function much better. A lot of that had to do with working so much. I didn't really have time to think about my mind as much and I wasn't around anyone my own age anymore to compare my life to so it wasn't as frustrating. I still wanted nothing more than to just go out to dinner with a girl, but I was still in no position to do that. I was a twenty five year old who lived with his mom and couldn't hold a steady job. Plus it had just been too long and I was sure my nervousness would just make a girl think I was weird and run away. I had to get my life together first and grow a little bit of confidence before I could even think about saying hi to a girl.

I kept working and kept thinking about L.A. but still couldn't decide if I was going back or not. I liked having money and keeping my mind busy enough with work so I wouldn't think about how alone I was. It sounds weird, but I liked not being around my friends because I wasn't seeing what I was missing. They were living the life I wanted and it was better if I separated myself from seeing that. I didn't want to go back and be the odd man out again, that was too hard.

I continued to just keep my head down and kept working for the next few months. Everything was going along fine and instead of trying to decide if I was going to move back or not, I just tried not to think about it at all. I was done trying to plan and just wanted to go along with what was happening and see where it took me.

As I was working at Desiderio, I spent a lot of time going in and out of a lot of different offices there changing light bulbs, moving stuff, or fixing things and never really noticed any of the people in them. I just went in, did what I was supposed to do and left without talking to any of them or anything. Then one day my uncle comes up to me and tells me some lady in one of the offices was asking about me and wanted to know if I was single. I thought he was joking and just kind blew it off because that seemed impossible. A few days later he told me she was asking about me again. Finally I started to believe him and went with him to her office and met her. She was a little bit older, shoulder length brunette hair, and was pretty attractive. Her name was Shayla and we talked for a while and although it was very awkward for me, I managed to muddle my way through it. I talked to her a few times more and then she actually asked me out. I wasn't planning on asking her out because I still found it hard to believe she liked me and I wouldn't have been able to put up with the rejection, but of course I agreed to go out with her. As I walked away from her office, I felt like a whole new man. I was excited for the first time in a long time and actually felt like being alive. I tried to not think about how awkward it was going to be going out with a girl for the first time in years and how I was going to have to force myself to be talkative and not come across as a depressed wreck, I only tried to focus on how good it felt to be going out on a date like a real boy.

We decided to meet at some restaurant and I showed up and sat at the bar and waited. Fifteen minutes later I was still waiting. I was about to accept the fact that I got stood up and go back home and kill myself, when the bartender came up to me and told me there was a call for me. It was her and she asked if I could meet her at another restaurant instead. I didn't ask why and just said yes and got back in my truck and thought about not going because it was turning out to be a lot more complicated than it should have been. I went to the other place anyway and met her and we had some food and some drinks and after a while of uncomfortable silence, it got better and we talked. She asked me if I had just gotten out of a relationship and I told her no, I hadn't even "been" with a girl in five years. She looked at me and said, "well we will have to change that!". I almost started crying I was so happy. We had a few more drinks to calm the nerves and then went back to her place where the impossible happened. Hell had frozen over and my virginity that had grown back because it had been so long, had once again been lost.

The next day I don't think there was anything that could wipe the smile off my face. I never felt so alive! I felt a little more normal and was able to look people in the eye instead of walking with my head down. It had been five years since I had felt that way. That was the longest five years of my life. That was harder to deal with than the homelessness, the constant struggle to pay bills, and maybe even the hunger. I was hoping that maybe that was exactly what I needed and I could "get the ball rolling", sort of speak. I figured I could at least go out with Shayla a few more times. She was really nice but it really didn't click personality wise and she knew that too. We went out again and then the counseling started. She told me how I have this wall/shield up all the time and I need to break it down and get over it. For an invisible shield, there sure were a lot of people that could see it and had to tell me about it. I was really tired of always hearing what was wrong with me and I just wanted a girlfriend, not a therapist. Anytime I would see her in her office it turned into a how to fix Travis class and it got really old really quick. I knew I was a mess and needed to change some things but I didn't need to constantly hear about it and be reminded of it, I was working on it on my own. I was the one that got me into my head, I wanted to be the one to get me out of it and I knew I could do it.

As time went on, I avoided her more and more because it was just getting to be too much and it was turning into one big Dr. Phil moment and lecture every time I saw her.

It wasn't too long after that Neal, my uncle, and me all left Desiderio. Not because of her, but for our own reasons. It started with my uncle. He had worked there for fifteen years or so and was still making the same hourly wage and Mrs. Desiderio was getting older, cheaper, and more controlling. She really started treating all of her employees like crap. Our hours were from 7:30 until 4:00 and out of nowhere she got all upset that we weren't on the job site and working until 7:45 or so. She wanted us to work from exactly 7:30 until 4:00, not stop at 3:30 and drive back to the shop and put tools away and be ready to leave at 4:00, but stop working at that time and then go put stuff away. It was a little weird to hear that all of a sudden, but that was fine and we did it. Until we realized we would not be getting paid for getting there early and staying late. We still would only be paid our eight hours. My uncle had a problem with that and threw a fit. The fit didn't help and we were expected to be at work at 7:00 to load up tools and everything in the truck and be at the job by 7:30 and not leave until exactly 4:00. We did that for a while and then she didn't trust us, so she made us punch a time card. That threw my uncle over the edge and it wasn't too long after that he quit and started his own thing.

Neal wasn't happy there either and soon he left to concentrate on his own business and I kind of had to quit to be able to work with Neal and mainly because I couldn't do all that stuff on my own and didn't want to try under those circumstances. She was about to lay me off anyway, so I just beat her to it. She was a horrible lady who treated everyone like crap and wasn't making much sense running her business anymore. She would spend a dollar just to save a dime as they say.

I still got to work for Neal from time to time but it wasn't very steady work. So, keeping with the theme of my life, it was the beginning of a new year and I was once again out of a job. I wasn't panicking as much as usual though because I still had some money saved up and was still living at my moms, but it was getting really old looking for a new job all the time.

I once again started the job search, wandering around applying everywhere, with no real prospects. I was still clueless on what I wanted to do and it didn't matter anyway, I just needed a job and was going to take anything I could get. I applied at all the casinos, restaurants, all the stores at the mall, and I heard nothing back from any of them for weeks. Same routine as always. I wasn't surprised anymore.

Then I got the call that 'On the Border' was hiring servers and I could come in for an interview. I went through my routine and got more and more nervous the closer I got to it and went in and asked for the manager. He came out and we sat down and I answered all the standard questions from the standard manager. He was just like all the others, but overall, the interview seemed to go pretty good considering it was me. He told me they would be hiring a group coming up in a week or two and it looked like he would be seeing me again. It wasn't my dream job, but I felt pretty good afterward.

Weeks went by and I had not heard anything so I gave him a call. He said he remembered me but decided to hire someone else instead. I didn't ask why or anything, I just thanked him and hung up.

I had a few more restaurant and retail interviews go pretty much the same way for the next couple of weeks and I was getting really, really tired of this routine and the managers attitudes. They were all the same person just in a different body. I had been on hundreds of interviews in L.A. and Reno now and I didn't know how much longer I could keep doing this. I hated this whole process and the people involved in it.

But I was starting to figure out that once you hit a point where it seems completely hopeless, something will come along to change it. You just have to be open minded and be willing to look for it.

I saw an article in the paper that said South Lake Tahoe was looking for on-call wildland firefighters and would be offering a free class coming up in a month. It was going to be first come first serve and if I didn't get in to that class I would have to take it at the college up at the lake. I knew what kind of luck I had, so I went and registered at the college just in case. I had no idea what being a wildland firefighter was all about, I thought the fire department took care of all that, but I figured it was something to look into and at least it was a change of pace from the restaurant and retail rejections I had dealing with for the last five years. I wasn't really putting all my eggs into one basket with this and it was still a month away with no guarantee that I would even get into the class, but it was something to look forward to.

It was now a few days until that class was about to start and I had an interview at the new P.F. Chang's that was just about to open. I really wanted to work there because I remembered how busy the one in L.A. was and I thought I would be able to make good money. I went into that interview thinking if I got the job, I wouldn't go to the firefighter class. If I didn't get the job, I would go to the class and never apply at any restaurant or retail place ever again. I would just go back to school or try to find some other job some other way because I could not keep going through this process.

The interview went much like the last hundred did. The manager was fake, condescending, and lied about how he was really looking forward to working with me because I did not get hired.

So firefighter class it was and I drove an hour and a half to get to it and was the first person there waiting at the door. I was easily an hour early but I wanted to make sure I got my spot. There ended up being about thirty people that made it into the class and I went in and got my seat. I was extremely nervous because I had no idea what any of this was. I didn't even know there were wildland firefighters and had no idea what they did. The class started and I was soon buried by paperwork and books. I sat there quietly and listened to everything that was said for the next few hours and then drove the hour and a half home. For the next four days, that was the routine. I would show up early just to make sure and then would sit in the class and learn what all of this firefighting was all about. The classes were long and there was a lot of information to take in, but when it came time to take the tests, I had no problem passing them.

After everyone finished taking the tests, they explained to us how we would be doing a field day the following day, physically doing all the things we had learned about all week. If we completed that, then we would be put on a waiting list and they would call the people they wanted when it was time for fire season.

The field day was long. It was very militaristic and we started out by doing the pack test which consisted of putting on a forty five pound vest and walking three miles in forty five minutes. It's not that hard, you can only walk, not run, but it's a fast pace and it makes you sweat. We then went hiking up a mountain and started clearing brush and digging a line around the pretend fire. It was steep and rocky, which made it very difficult to dig in, but I just kept my head down and kept digging. We continued that for an hour or so and it was exhausting. We then went back down the hill and learned how to hand sharpen all the tools we destroyed hitting all of the rocks. That was exhausting too. We then went through a scenario where the fire was chasing us and we had to get into our fire shelters. We had to run full speed and then pull out the shelter from our pack and get into it and lay there for a while and it was a little claustrophobic and I swallowed a lot of dirt. If shit ever hit the fan and we couldn't outrun the fire, we would have to get into this tin foil tarp looking thing and wrap up in it and let the fire go by, so we practiced that at least a dozen times. It was exhausting.

We learned a few more little things and then they told us to stay by the phone and they might call us at any time. With that, it was over and I went home, showered, fell asleep and doubted I would ever hear from them again.

A week or two went by and no one called and I was still out of a job. One of my moms friends offered to pay me to dig up her lawn and take it to the dump, so I agreed and started in on that. About half way through the job I got the call. They told me to show up the next day at the South Lake Airport and bring a lunch and enough socks and underwear for fourteen days. That's all they would tell me. I just stood there with my mouth open after I hung up because I did not know what was going on. Was I flying somewhere to a fire or were we driving or were we just meeting, what was going on!? I finished digging up most of the lawn and took it to the dump, which was amazing because I was so nervous and my mind was racing so fast I thought I was going to pass out. I had no idea what I was getting into the next day and that was a scary feeling.

I didn't sleep much that night and the next morning I drove to the airport and saw about fifteen people waiting around. I got out of my car and as I started walking up to them, it felt like my first Pop Warner football practice all over again. Here were all of these tough looking guys that wanted to be firefighters and here I am all awkward and in my coke bottle glasses because they told me not to wear my contacts. I was so nervous my stomach hurt and once I got the courage to ask some people what was going on, I found out that none of them knew anything and they were all just as nervous as I was. That made me feel a little better at least. I still wanted to know what was going on.

Then a big old white school bus pulls into the parking lot along with a Forest Service pick up truck behind it. Two burly, manly looking men get out of the truck and tell us to get our stuff and load it up onto the bus. Everyone grabs their garbage bags full of socks and underwear and piles onto the bus and we start driving without knowing where we are going. A few minutes later we arrive at the same place we had our field day and we are told to line up and get all of our shirts, pants, and all of our gear and put our garbage bag full of stuff into the big red bag they were going to give us. Finally after all of that, they explained some things to us like this:

We will meet everyday at the airport and work ten hour days for fourteen days straight before we get two days off. That will be our schedule–fourteen on, two off, for the rest of the fire season. We will work around Lake Tahoe doing forestry work until we get called to a fire, which could be at any time, so have all of your stuff ready to go at all times. The big white bus will be our transportation and home all season and is appropriately named Great White. Respect Great White. If you want a day off or call in sick, we will replace you with one of the many people waiting for this opportunity who haven't been called yet. This is your foot in the door to a career in firefighting, if you act like you don't want to be here, we will find someone who does. If you don't think you can handle it, leave now so we can get someone else.

That told us just about everything we needed to know. I wasn't sure if I was going to be able to handle it, but I needed the job and nothing had ever been easy for me when I first started it, so I would have just have to see.

We had just sat down to lunch and were told to load up on the bus to go to a fire. My stomach dropped. It was only a couple hours into our very first day and I had no idea how to even wear all of my gear correctly yet. We started driving and they told us we were going to the El Dorado

National Forest. I had no idea where that was. I thought I was nervous before, but that was nothing to what I was going through now.

After about a two hour drive, I looked out the window and saw the plume of smoke shadowing the sun. I couldn't believe that's where we were going. As we got closer and made our way through all the dirt roads, I saw a bunch of fire engines and trucks with their lights on and we parked right next to them and got out, put our packs on, grabbed our tools, lined up in single file order and followed the boss up the mountain. It was steep and a lot more tiring than I thought it was going to be just getting up the hill. I thought I was in pretty good shape but I had never done any hiking before and it just about killed me. We kept on hiking and the higher we got up on the mountain, the darker and smokier it was getting and all of our eyes were huge when we saw what seemed to be the entire forest on fire. We kept walking up and it kept getting hotter and darker, my legs kept getting weaker, and the fire kept getting bigger. It was as loud as a freight train and all I could hear were trees falling, tanker planes zooming by, and helicopters overhead. Finally we made it to where we were supposed to start in and a couple of the only guys that had been on the crew before started up their chain saws and started cutting brush and tree limbs like mad men. I remember looking at them in amazement wondering how they knew what to cut and how do I get to be able to do that? We had to wait for the saws to get ahead a little bit and I stood there and looked around and probably didn't blink the whole time. Everything was on fire and I had no idea where I was. Fifty foot trees were going up in flames and it looked like we were surrounded by fire to me. I thought about how the day before I was unemployed digging out some lady's lawn for a few bucks and twenty four hours later I was here, wherever here was, on a mountain that was on fire and trusting these people that I had only met a few hours before.

It was now time for us to follow where the saws had cut and start digging a line around the fire. They had given me a Pulaski and I had no clue as what to do with it, I just did what the guy in front of me did. I kept digging and digging as hard as I could. The flames were so hot I felt my lips chap instantly, sweat was pouring off of me, the smoke was burning my eyes, and my arms were cramping up from digging so hard. What the hell did I get myself into?

After what seemed like forever, we had completed our line around what turned out to only be a one acre spot fire and we got to sit down and rest. The sun had gone down and I couldn't see anything except black and orange now. What we had just put line around seemed so small compared to everything else that was burning. As we sat there, all I could hear were trees falling and I was so hungry and tired I didn't even care. I hadn't eaten since lunch, about ten hours before, and I don't think I had ever burned that many calories at once before. I was starting to feel a little sick from hunger and all the smoke I had sucked in, but it wasn't too bad yet. After we checked our spot fire and made sure it was secure, we headed back down the mountain back to Great White.

It was around ten o'clock now and they told us we were headed back down to camp. I didn't even know what that meant, I thought we were done. We loaded our tools and ourselves onto the bus and began to drive. About fifteen minutes into the drive I started feeling really sick. So sick I was going to puke. I was smashed in the middle of the bus next to a couple guys that were sleeping so I couldn't exactly ask to pull over, so I puked in the little cooler I had brought my lunch in. It was bad and I just wanted to go to sleep.

We arrived at the camp, which was just a flat spot in the woods, and they had California inmates there cooking dinner. We got our food and sat down and ate it. I tried to eat it at least. I was still pretty nauseous and although I was starving, I just couldn't get it down. After a few bites I gave up on eating for the night and waited to be told where we could sleep.

After a not so good nights rest on the ground in a sleeping bag, we woke up at five, had some inmate breakfast that I was able to keep down, and headed back to the fire. When we got there, we parked in the same spot and hiked up the same way and it was just as tiring. The fire wasn't as active and once we made it to the top, we started mopping up. I didn't know how to do that either, but I asked a few questions and eventually understood the concept. We worked until ten that night and went back to camp and now that I wasn't nauseous, the food was pretty good. We went to sleep and woke up at five and did it all over again for the next two days.

When it was time to go back home, I couldn't have been happier. My feet were killing me, my legs felt like noodles, and pretty much my whole body hurt from digging and not sleeping much. I couldn't wait to take a shower either, I had never gone four days without showering before, even when I was homeless.

So that was my very first fire. It was named the Nevada fire and was started by loggers. It turned out to be twenty five acres total. We spent four days there and I hated every minute of it. We went back home and had to be at work the next day and for the next ten days until we could have a day off. I kept showing up and was starting to see that this job had no excuses. There was no leaving early, no taking sick days, and no complaining. That was a refreshing change and I liked it. Everyone just showed up to work everyday, worked hard doing physically demanding work, and never complained about it. Even though I didn't think I was cut out for this job, I knew I needed to be around that kind of attitude and work ethic, so I kept showing up.

For the next ten days we did tree thinning work around Lake Tahoe. The sawyers would go around and cut down trees and cut them up into movable pieces and we would stack them into piles so in the winter they could burn them. It was extremely boring and tiring work. Ten hours a day of nothing but picking up logs and branches and stacking them into piles and I again doubted if I was going to be able to do this. I figured I had to make it to my days off at least and until then I would just work as hard as I possibly could. It paid off because one day as I was stacking sticks, the boss called me over to his truck. Of course with my complete lack of self confidence, I thought I was in trouble. He told me I was doing one hell of a job at all of this and I was one of the hardest workers he had seen in a long time and to keep up the good work. Wasn't expecting that! That made my day and I put all the doubt I had about doing this job in the back of my head. It was a good confidence boost and that was exactly what I needed.

On our fourteenth straight day of work, everyone was excited to finally have two days off. It was down to the last hour or so of work for the day and everyone was antsy and staring at their watch and getting all of their stuff together to take home and wash so it would all be ready when we came back. The bosses then called us all over to gather up and told us that there were so many people on the waiting list to get onto the crew that they had to rotate some of us out and we would not be coming back after our days off. That was never mentioned before and it came as a huge surprise. I, along with everyone else, just stood there and couldn't believe it. They told us if anyone wanted to volunteer to leave it would be appreciated and it would give them a better chance of getting back on the crew later on. No one volunteered so they told us they would go decide who was going to leave and let us know before we left. I wasn't sure if I was going to get picked to leave or not. The boss told me how good of a job I was doing and there were a lot of other people that didn't seem as motivated as I was, but then again I knew my luck with jobs and a two week job seemed like it was right around the average for me, so it was hard to predict.

Luckily they only told five people to leave and I was not one of them. It was sad to see those guys go against their will, but it was also relieving to know that I had at least two more weeks of work. After seeing who they let go, I knew I had to work even harder the next two weeks just to keep my job, even though it looked like only a matter of time before I would have to leave so someone else could get a chance.

The weeks went by, we kept going to fires, I kept working my ass off to keep my job, and I was never asked to leave. Before I knew it, fire season was over and only me and two other guys had made it through the whole season. On our last day they told me I was one of the first picked to be on the crew because I was always the first one to class and I always kept my mouth shut and I was kept on the crew because I kept working harder and harder every week and I always kept my mouth shut. Be on time, work hard, and keep my mouth shut. Got it.

My first fire season was a good one and I learned more and changed more from it than any other thing I had ever done. I was more tolerant and learned not to make excuses or complain about my job. If I didn't like it, go somewhere else, otherwise just keep my mouth shut and work hard and make the best of it. I also had a goal with the job, a first for any job I had ever had. I wanted to move up on the crew and be a sawyer. They were kind of like the unofficial leaders of a crew because they had to be in better shape to carry the saw around all day and had to be trusted to be safe with a saw and to be able to be on their own more than the people with tools. I wanted to do that and thought if I came back to the same crew the following year, I would have a better opportunity to do that. Although this was a beginning level crew, I still wanted to come back and take it one step at a time. First learn how to be a sawyer, then go to a more established crew, then end up being a sawyer on a hot shot crew. That was the top for me at the time and I wanted to see if I could do it. But I couldn't get ahead of myself, I had to take it one step at a time, I wasn't even sure if I could get back on the crew the next year.

I now had six months before fire season started again but had saved enough money to not panic. I was still living at my moms and was still undecided if I was going back to L.A. or not and it was coming up on my twenty seventh birthday. I needed to make a decision. Although living at my moms was great, I didn't want to be twenty seven and still living there. I went back and forth on it for a while more and then one day just got in my truck and went apartment hunting. The first complex I stopped at was nice and had a place available so I took it. Just like that. I went and told my mom and although she was sad to see me move out of her place, she was happy I wasn't going back to L.A. I never came right out and said I wasn't going to move back, but getting my own place in Reno pretty much said it loud and clear.

I still wanted to move back though, but things were going pretty good and for the first time ever I felt like I was getting my shit together. I never talked about my plans, even back in high school and college, and this time was no different. In the back of my mind, I was planning on spending another year in Reno and doing another year of firefighting and then moving back to L.A. I thought about how I might be able to get a fire job down there and everything would be set. I kept it to myself though and tried not to think too far ahead or carve it in stone because I knew my plans very rarely went according to plan. For the moment, I just needed to concentrate on moving into my new apartment and making sure I was going to get hired back onto the crew for the next fire season.

13

IT WAS NICE to have my own place again, even if it was in Reno. After I got settled in, it wasn't long before it started feeling like home. My stuff had spent so much time in storage or in my moms garage for the last few years, it was nice to have it all out where I could see it and use it.

The longer I lived there, the more the fantasy of moving back to L.A. faded away. I was really tired of moving and it was really nice to have my place and my stuff in it and have something to look forward to in a job. It was also really nice to be around my mom and my uncle. I would work with him from time to time helping him with his new home repair and remodeling business he started. He worked by himself and I didn't work with him very much, only when he needed another body, but it was nice to work with him even if it was just a little bit.

Like I said, I never talked about my plans and I never told anyone that I was now planning on just staying in Reno. It was just so much easier in Reno and I was so tired of starting over and struggling and I was getting too old to still not have a clue what I was doing in life. It was sad to accept I wouldn't move back to L.A. anytime soon. I loved living there even though I spent a good amount of time struggling, and no one seems to understand that. They think it was the city that beat me down, but it was me and my own mind, not the city. I would have struggled anywhere with a mind as messed up as mine was then. I loved everything about the city: the weather, the people(except douche bag wannabe actors), the diversity, the scenery, the energy, everything. Reno was and always will be my hometown, but L.A. felt like my home. I was going to miss it there, but like a lot of things, I was just going to have to try and not let it get to me and move forward.

I did go back and visit Arnold in our old apartment once though and it was weird. After I had moved out, he had gotten two roommates to move in and they were gay. That wasn't the weird part, I have no problem with that, it was just weird to see my room looking so different and to have it lived in by someone else. I slept on the couch and what used to be my home, now felt awkward and like I was in the way.

I went back because I had nothing going on and he and some of his friends were making a short film and I could hang around and watch and be an extra in it. I spent a few days there and it was great. I hung out at the coffee place like I used to and then I would go and watch them make the film. It was cool to hang around all of that and to be an extra and it got me regretting that I didn't really try to pursue acting more. The last night shooting the movie was at a bar and we spent all night there until the sun came up. Afterward, they all wanted to go to breakfast and hang out and I knew it would be too awkward for me and I would be criticized for being so quiet, so I saved myself the embarrassment and just went to the apartment. When I got there, the guard wouldn't let me in. He had let me in the last three days, but for some reason, not now. I was tired and just wanted to go to sleep and I couldn't get in. I tried to call Arnold so he could tell them to let me in, but he didn't have his phone on because he was working. I went to coffee and waited and about an hour later, Arnold called back and told me he called the guy and he would let me in now. That apartment and their security guards had not changed in years. When I first moved there, they wouldn't let me in, and now after three days straight of seeing me and letting me in, they changed their minds. The next morning I left and drove back to Reno. L.A. just wasn't the same if I couldn't live there.

It was getting close to the start of a new fire season and all I had to do was take a one day class to be able to have a chance of getting on the crew again. I took the class and soon after was called to be on the crew. Right away, I was taught about being a sawyer and was soon falling trees and humping a saw around with me everywhere I went. I liked having a saw a lot better than a tool because I had to constantly be aware. I couldn't just go on auto pilot and zone out or I would ruin my chain by hitting a rock or ruin my life by cutting my leg off.

My second fire season went well and I was glad I came back and learned the saw but it felt like it was time to move on to a more established crew. This crew was a starting point. It was an all rookie crew and they didn't want people to be on it more than two seasons. Other crews got to go on more fires, got hazard pay, got overtime pay, and their season was longer and more stable. This crew was just a bunch of beginners thrown together and it all could have ended after any of the two week periods without warning. The other crews were on until the end of fire season no matter what. So that was my next goal, get on a "real" crew.

After the fire season, my uncle was starting to get pretty busy with his business and needed more and more help so that became my winter job. It was a pretty nice set up I had going, firefighting in the summer and working for him in the winter getting paid cash. I had my own place and it really looked like I had my shit together finally. I even got a bug up my butt and decided to take a class at the community college again. I was kind of thinking about trying to get on with the fire department and thought I should take a couple classes to maybe help with that. I wasn't going to go through all the bullshit and try to buy a degree, but I just wanted to take some random classes and started out by taking First Responder. I took that class at night and worked with my uncle during the day and that was my life that winter.

Another reason I wanted to take the classes was to keep my mind occupied so I wouldn't just sit at home all night thinking about how lonely I was. I had absolutely no friends in Reno and I knew even if I did, I wouldn't have fit in anyway. I still wanted to be able to fit in though and if I thought about it too much, I would feel the depression settling in, so I had to keep my mind off of it.

I finished my class and got an A in it, shocking for me. Another fire season was right around the corner and I started applying on the website for any crews that would take me. While I was waiting to hear from any of them, my uncle's business was really doing well and he was busy. It looked like he would have enough work to keep both him and me busy throughout the summer and offered me to work with him instead of doing fire. It was something to think about. Firefighting was good for me and I wanted to keep doing it, but it would be nice to have a job where I got to go home every night and make more per hour and it would be easier on my body. I also really liked working with him, all we did was giggle like a couple of teenage girls the whole time we worked, so it was more fun than climbing a mountain with a saw over my shoulder all summer. I thought about it for a while and although I doubted my decision making ability, I figured I would make one more bad decision and change my job again and see if it would work out.

It turned out to not be a bad decision at all and we kept busy and it was a good summer. It was nice to have a summer after spending the last two climbing around a burning forest the whole time. I would go to work in the morning, go to the gym after work, then go home and enjoy the summer evenings just like a real person. It was really nice and it made me want to keep doing this kind of work instead of fire so I could be home more, even though I had no real reason to be home.

It was somewhere around this time that my mom had gotten a second wiener dog. Bandit and Bucky had been in doggy heaven for a while now and she had Washoe, my dog Nikki, and Lewis but couldn't resist a free wiener dog puppy that needed a home. One of the guys she works with gave it to her and she named him Leo, after that guy. It took a while for Lewis to warm up to him, but they became big buds and it was so cute watching them run around together. Animals make our lives so much better.

During that summer, my uncle was really getting into motorcycles and he was doing so well with his business that he went and bought himself one. I always wanted one ever since I was little, but never said anything because I figured I would be told that it was stupid and I would kill myself on one. My aunt was a helicopter flight nurse and saw a lot of motorcycle accident victims so she hated them. Of course she saw a lot of things and thought that anything that *could* be dangerous should just be avoided. I never understood that kind of thinking. You could get hurt or killed doing anything. You could slip and fall in the shower, doesn't mean you should avoid taking showers. Living a life where you constantly avoid doing things for fear of dying is no way to live.

So after he got his bike, he had to take the class to get his license and I went and took it with him, even though I had no intentions of ever getting a bike myself. I just went for moral support and it sounded like it might be fun. We went to Carson City and sat through the class the first night and it was cool. We had plenty of people to make fun of and we were excited to be able to learn how to ride the next two days. The next morning we went out on the course and learned how to ride and did a bunch of "exercises" to get us ready for the riding test the next day. My uncle did well and I did well for the most part. I had trouble with one of the tight turn drills, but everything else went well. We finished up the day and looked forward to taking both the written and the riding test the next day and getting our licenses.

The next day came around and we started by doing the riding test. The first few parts went well and it seemed like no problem. As the day went on, it got hotter and hotter. It was the middle of summer and we were out on the blacktop in long sleeves and gloves and the heat started getting to Martin. I was used to it, but it really got to him and he wasn't able to complete one of the drills and didn't pass the riding test. I somehow was able to do the tight turn part with no issues and I passed. We then went inside and took the written part and we both passed but he still couldn't get his license. It was rather awkward. I just went to keep him company, he was the one who had a bike and needed the license, not me. So it was a long ride home and he was pretty bummed out about it and I was bummed for him.

A month or two went by and I kept looking at the big M on my license and really started wanting a motorcycle. I looked around for a while and got more and more hopped up about it the more I looked at them. That riding class was the first time I had ever been on one and it was a lot of fun and I couldn't get it out of my head. I told my mom about it and I thought she might be against it, but she was all for it and offered to help buy one. I couldn't afford a fancy chopper like my uncle had gotten, but I found one that was cheaper and that I really liked the looks of. It was short and fat like me and was reasonably priced just like me. I took my mom down to the shop and I took the plunge. I got a Suzuki cruiser and was so excited I almost wet myself. When it was time to take it home, I'm pretty sure I did wet myself. I had never driven a bike on a real road with other cars on it before, and it was a little scary at first. I pulled out onto the busy street and I felt naked out there. Everyone was driving so fast and I was just out there with no big metal box around me. My mom followed me back home and I think I hit a top speed of 30 mph on a 50 mph street. I was nervous and didn't want to go any faster and eventually I made it home safe and sound. I put the bike away and then needed a nap. It had been a big day for me.

Although Martin still didn't have a license, he still rode it and when I told him I had gotten a bike too, he was excited to have someone to ride with. I was excited too, I loved just zooming around town on my bike and it was nice to have someone to go with. It was my new hobby and I couldn't get enough of it. I slowly got more comfortable on it and eventually was able to keep up with traffic. Once it was time to start going to classes at the college again, I rode it there every time I could and life was good. Work during the day, then go and ride my bike to class, then take the longest way home possible afterward and do it all over again the next day. It would have been a good time to have a girlfriend, but I couldn't think about that. It didn't seem possible for me.

I was now taking three more classes at the college. I took Nutrition, Spanish, and the Entry Level Firefighter for structure firefighting. The fire class was only for a few weekends in a row so it wasn't as busy as it sounds, but busy enough to keep my mind occupied. The classes went well and I got an A in all of them and I got out of them what I wanted. The fire class really made me want to get a job with the fire department but I thought I should get some more experience in wildland first before I would try since it was so competitive to get hired.

It was starting to slow down a lot at work with my uncle and I figured I had better apply with some fire crews just in case things didn't pick up. I applied with everyone and some called me to see if I was going to school or not since fire season starts in April or so and classes don't get done until the middle of May. After I told them I was going to school, I never heard back from them. I understood, but it seemed ironic. That really didn't help my faith in the whole schooling system. So I was planning on just working with my uncle when needed and hopefully things would pick up and I would have a steady job again. They never did, but out of nowhere, a crew from Truckee called me and asked if I would be available after I was done with my classes. I said yes and I was hired. They were one of the crews that I had talked to before but didn't hire me because I couldn't be there full time for a few weeks. For some reason, now they were ready for me so I didn't question it and was ready to go.

My first day was just like all of my other first days, awkward. Although all but one guy was new to the crew that year, I was still a couple of weeks behind and I was the new guy. I hate being the new guy. We did a lot of classroom training and a lot of physical training for the first few weeks and that was all knew to me. It seemed so much more organized and we had so much better gear and tools to work with than the last crew. This crew was trying to become a hot shot crew and I thought it would be perfect to start now and stick with it and be part of the transition. The crew was called Truckee Hand Crew and was a very respected Type 2 crew and I was put on as a sawyer after they had "try outs". That was a pretty big deal to me because it meant that I stood out and was in good enough shape.

I learned a lot that year. If we weren't on a fire, we were in the classroom learning and training and I felt like I was really starting to understand firefighting better and what it took to do it. I learned how much tougher it was to be on a real crew than the rookie one. We would run and train a lot harder and a lot more than the other crew did. The fires we went to were bigger and more complex and it was a lot more hiking to get to them.

We went to a fire in the Klamath National Forest one time and it was around 90 degrees and the humidity was up around 40%. Lightning had gone through the night before and started about fifty different fires. The one we got assigned to was out in the middle of nowhere. We were to grab enough food and water for three days and hike up to the fire. The hike ended up being a six hour hike and right around hour four, I started feeling weird. I had about sixty pounds on my back, ten more than I was used to because of the extra food and water, and I started sweating profusely because of the humidity. I kept going as long as I could but eventually I had to stop and people had to cool me off. I was used to desert heat and no humidity and this stuff was really getting to me. I felt like crap but after a good rest, I was up and able to finish the hike. We got to the fire and started in and worked throughout the night. We then got a good three hours of sleep and went back at it the next day. We spent a few days up there and then were helicoptered out and went to another one. It was exhausting and I was embarrassed that I fell out of the hike. I was always one of the best hikers and fastest runners on the crew and this really was a blow to my ego. The day after I was back to normal and that was the only time it happened all year, but I still felt like a wimp and thought about it a lot.

I didn't fit in with the snowboarding, pot smoking, Tahoe group that was on the crew but I didn't really care, I was there to work and get a paycheck, not make friends. Most of them would hang out together when we weren't on fires and I never did. I got a lot of shit for that, but I didn't want to get involved with all of that. I never liked hanging out with people I worked with. People are different outside of work and I didn't want to know that part of them. I would be friendly to them at work and all, but I wanted to separate myself from work when I wasn't at work. Besides, I would spend fourteen, sometimes twenty one days straight with these people. I would eat, sleep and work next to them, every minute of everyday, I didn't want to spend my days off with them too.

My third fire season and first on a real crew went well and I made more money than I had ever made before, although that isn't saying much. I learned a lot and was planning on coming back the next season in even better shape and becoming a better sawyer. We never got to try to become a hot shot crew that year but I knew we would get the chance to soon. Even if we didn't get the chance I was going to stay on this crew for a while. I liked it, I made more money, and it was only a half hour drive away from home, which was a lot better than the hour and half each way I took to get to South Lake Tahoe.

Although it was a good, respectable job and I was planning on going back, it did suck that I never got to ride my new motorbike. I only had a couple of days off every month and by the time fire season was over, it was too cold to ride. At least I had a job and wasn't broke and homeless anymore. Can't have it all I guess.

My winter months consisted of recovering and working with my uncle when he needed help. It was enough work to make me some money but not so much that I was exhausted, so it was a nice set up. Other than that, it was a pretty uneventful time. I was still lonely and had nothing to look forward to except torturing myself with another fire season.

One day I saw that I had an email from one of my mom's assistants that used to work for her. Her name was Gina and she had since moved on and worked at a bank now, but they still remained friends. She was one of my mom's favorite assistants that she ever had and I remember my mom telling me all about her and how funny she was. I had only seen her a few times when I went to see my mom at work and I always thought she was cute, but she was married, so I thought nothing of it. I remember my mom telling me that Gina had gotten a divorce a while back but I still didn't think anything of it because I didn't think I stood a chance. I didn't even think she knew I existed because every time I saw her in the office, she would just say hi and then immediately leave.

Her email basically told me that she was divorced now and if I ever wanted to go get a beer with her, just as friends, to give her a call. I didn't quite know what to think. I really didn't think she knew I existed and

I really wasn't expecting that. I was excited because a girl was actually asking me out to do something, even if it was just as friends. But of course I started to over think everything and could only think about how uncomfortable it would be for me if I did go out with her. I had only gone out with one girl in the last decade and I would have nothing to talk about and I would be completely self conscious and I would just end up embarrassing myself and then she would start telling me what was wrong with me and how I needed to change and then she would tell my mom how much of a freak I was and then my mom would make fun of me and it would just turn into this big ordeal that would make me want to crawl under a rock and hide for the rest of my life. So long story short, I didn't call her but I replied to her email and basically told her that we would go out sometime and I would call her. I never did call her though. I really wanted to and almost did a few times, but I chickened out and decided to not humiliate myself.

Some time went by and I still didn't have the courage to dial her number. I figured she had probably forgotten about me by now anyway. I continued being lonely and then one day I answered the phone and it was my old boss Neal's wife. She tried to explain who she was, but it had been so long since I had seen him or her that I thought it was the wrong number. I finally figured it out and she told me she had gotten a divorce from him a couple of years ago and wanted to know if I wanted to hang out. This was weird. First Gina emailing me out of the blue and now this girl? I felt so popular! I politely declined for much of the same reasons as I did with Gina. She would not give up though and kept calling and calling until I finally agreed. We met for coffee I think, and it was fine. She was a talker so it didn't matter that I wasn't and I wasn't very nervous around her because I really wasn't attracted to her. Nothing wrong with her, but it just wasn't "it". A few nights later she came over with dinner and although I wasn't into her, I am a guy and it had been four years(for the second time) since I had been with anyone, so for the second time in the last decade, I got lucky. I once again was a huge slut and felt a little bit of my confidence grow back. I was a womanizer now!

We went out a couple more times and then I just couldn't take it anymore. Even though I was a womanizer, I still couldn't lie to myself. I didn't like her and I didn't want to see her anymore. There was absolutely no connection and even though I had imagined and wished to be with someone for the last four years, it really wasn't worth it. I told her it was just too weird and I didn't see this going anywhere. I also threw in that I would be gone all summer on fires and that would be too tough. I told her everything except what I wanted to say: that no matter how much I wanted to get "lucky", it wasn't worth it because I didn't like her. My womanizer card was soon revoked.

She kept calling but we never went out again and soon the calls were fewer and fewer. I felt like an idiot, I was so lonely and wanted nothing more than to be with someone and here I was shooting down someone who wanted to be with me. I guess it never occurred to me that I had to actually like the person. I guess I had to be more specific than just wishing to be with someone. Be careful what you wish for.

It was now only about a month before fire season started and even with my new found confidence, I was still too nervous to call Gina so I just figured it was never going to happen. That is when she sent me another email. The timing in which things happen in life is exactly how it is supposed to go. Everything happens for a reason and only when you are ready for it to happen.

She invited me to go out and have a beer with her again and gave me her number and told me to call her if I wanted to. I think it took a few days to get the guts to do it but I eventually did call her. I was very nervous and just made a bunch of stupid jokes that she politely laughed at and we ended up talking on the phone for an hour or so. It was great. One of the best and easiest conversations I had ever had. She was funny, had the same sense of humor and had the cutest voice I had ever heard. I agreed to go have a beer with her and we planned on meeting at a bar called Luckies. After I hung up the phone, I was so happy and excited I just paced around my apartment for an hour.

On the drive over to meet her at the bar, I realized I should have brought a change of shirt because I had already pitted out the one I had on from nerves. I really didn't want to make an ass out of myself and I really didn't want it to end up being a therapy session for me. Somehow I knew it wouldn't be, just from being on the phone with her, but you never know. As I pulled up to the bar I got really nervous. I had not seen her in years and didn't know if she still looked the same or what and I hate being the guy who walks in somewhere and stands there while the whole place turns around and looks at him while he looks around to try and find the person he is meeting and has that stupid look on his face while the person he is looking for is staring right at him but he sees everything and everyone except that person and continues to stand there all lost and confused until the person finally stands up and waves and then he feels like an idiot and gets that relieved, embarrassed look and tries to play it off. I hate being that guy.

So I play it off like I saw her the whole time and go sit down next to her. She looked different than I remembered but was also even cuter than I remembered. I ordered a beer and we talked. About what, I don't remember, I was too nervous and self conscious about my pit stained shirt. I remember it didn't take long though before we started to relax and were able to talk without it seeming forced and it was going really good, for me at least. We had a few more beers and my pits slowed down from a steady stream to a slow drip and I was starting to feel comfortable around her. I asked her why she emailed me and she admitted that she always had a crush on me and when I used to come into the office, she would get all embarrassed and have to leave. I always thought I just smelled or something. I told her how I always thought she was cute but she was married, so I didn't think anything of it. That kind of broke the ice a little bit more and for the rest of the night we were kind of flirting with each other. We decided to go play pool and when we stood up, I saw how much taller she was than me. Of course just about everyone is taller than me, but this time it didn't bother me. Usually being the short guy just egged on my insecurities, but for once it didn't bother me. I thought she was really cool and I was having a good time and it just didn't matter. We played pool for a while and flirted for a while longer.

We ended up staying at the bar for hours but it didn't seem that long. Before I knew it, it was midnight or so and it was time to call it a night. I knew I wanted to go out with her again and it seemed like she could at least tolerate me, so I think we planned to go out together the next night. I walked her to her car and asked for a ride to my truck, which was only about fifty feet away. I got in and after the ten second road trip, it was time for me to get out. Then I went in and kissed her, something I never thought I would be able to do. That was way outside my comfort zone, but I just wanted to. I really liked her and had to see what would happen. Luckily she kissed me back and didn't throw up afterward, so that was nice. We giggled like ten year olds and then I got in my truck and went home. I smiled the entire drive home and couldn't wait to see her again.

The second time we got together was just as great. She came over to my apartment and I think we had pizza and watched 'Happy Feet'. It was a good night but my nerves were back and I was a little more reserved than before. There were some uncomfortable silences and I was afraid that I was going to screw this up with my insecurities. As the night went on, she looked like she wanted to say something. She finally asked me why I had not kissed her hello or had not tried to kiss her at all the whole night. I was wondering that as well. I really wasn't sure if she wanted me to or not. In my mind, I'm always doubting myself and find it hard to believe that anybody would want me to kiss them. I didn't want to be too pushy and ruin it I guess. I didn't know if she was looking to be in a relationship with me or not, she had just gotten out of one with some guy that treated her like crap, so I wasn't sure if she just wanted a friend and we just kissed the first night because of the liquid courage we both drank. I felt bad that I didn't kiss her though, I wanted to. I really liked her but I was so inexperienced at all of this dating stuff, I wasn't sure what I was supposed to do. I tried to be as honest as I could without sounding like too much of a freak and that helped and the rest of the night went great.

We started going out on a regular basis and I could not have been happier. The more I got to know her, the more I liked her. She was cute, funny, loved her family and animals, and I just wanted to be with her as much as possible. She was really the first girl I had ever felt comfortable around and who didn't tell me what was wrong with me and didn't try to change me. We just had fun together and the more time I spent with her, the more I was falling for her. She actually made me like myself. That is the biggest compliment I can give anyone.

I remember the first time I met her parents. It was at a country bar and that was good because it was loud and we couldn't talk much. I was so nervous to meet them and didn't want to say anything wrong or make an ass out of myself. I had never really met any girls parents before so I didn't know what I was supposed to do or say. They then invited me out to dinner a few nights later. Once again, I should have brought a change of shirt with me, because it didn't take long for me to pit out the one I had on. Even though I had met them once before, this time was in a quiet restaurant where I would have to talk. I was scared as hell to really meet her dad. I never had a dad and never met any girls dads and I did not know how to act. I was uncomfortable around men to begin with, but now that it was the father of the girl I really liked, I was even more uncomfortable if at all possible. I just wanted him to like me and I didn't want to get the usual criticism for being so quiet. I was nervous about meeting her mom, Whitney, as well but even Gina was more worried about me meeting her dad, so of course that is what I focused on.

It turned out to be a very nice night. Her mom was one of the nicest, sweetest people I had ever met and her dad was not at all judgmental or did not attempt to be intimidating over me like I had heard some fathers can be. He asked me a lot of questions about firefighting which was good because I knew what I was talking about and he was very, very nice to me. Afterward I didn't know what I was so nervous about because I really liked her parents a lot and they seemed to not hate me, so it was a big relief. I think Gina was more nervous than anyone though.

Fire season was right around the corner now and I was just finishing up my EMT class I had been taking. That was the only class I took that semester but it was a four hour class, two nights a week and I had to work in the emergency room a couple of times, so it kept me busy. I finished the class with an A, my fourth A in a row, something I never thought would happen, but I still had to take the National Registry to get certified. I had to wait until my grades and everything went through the computer system and then make an appointment to take the final test at some building across town. The only problem with that was I only had six months to take the test and fire season had already begun. I couldn't make an appointment because I never knew when I would be gone on a fire. I tried to take it right away but I had to wait for my info to go through the computer and by the time they did, I was gone on a fire. By the end of fire season, I had missed the deadline to take the test and I never got officially certified. It sucked because I needed that to apply with fire departments and I wanted to take the next level of EMT. It was ironic, I couldn't apply to be a firefighter because I was too busy being a firefighter.

My fourth fire season was a good one. I was one of the top runners and hikers on the crew and didn't have anymore overheating issues. I was getting better with the saw, better with the understanding of firefighting, and a better attitude. I had more confidence because I had some good experience as a firefighter now and I had a girlfriend, so it was all really coming together for me.

I wanted to stay on the crew until we became hot shots, but I didn't know if I was going to make it. It was tough and the bosses kept getting tougher and tougher on us. They would work us until people would be falling over or getting hurt. A few guys got dehydrated because they would tell us to conserve our water. I may have been new to this, but I knew that was wrong. It's ninety degrees out with a raging fire making it even hotter, we are working our asses off digging and swinging a saw for sixteen hours straight, we are going to need some water.

They started working us that hard even when we weren't on a fire. We would spend all morning working our asses off and then we would get called to a fire and everyone would be dead on their feet when we got there. We weren't allowed to have the air conditioning on while we drove and we were constantly lectured about everything, even drinking too much water. I know they were just trying to toughen us up, but at some point it just isn't safe anymore. They told us we had to be tougher if we were going to be a hot shot crew and I didn't know any better so I just kept at it and tried to get tougher. I wanted to reach my goal of being a sawyer on a hot shot crew.

Fire season had been going along now for about five months and my relationship with Gina had been going on about the same. I was so happy being with her and couldn't wait to see her every chance I got. Fire season kind of got in the way of that because I would be gone for two or three weeks at a time and then be home for only a day or two before I left again. That sucked and I was hoping she would be able to make it through the rest of the season and I was actually considering working on an engine the following year instead of the crew so I could be home more and spend more time with her. I was really wishing I would have been with her back when I worked with my uncle and got to go home every night and have weekends off. That would have been perfect.

It was nearing the end of the season, maybe a month and a half left and we went to a fire in Northern California. It looked like we would be there for at least fourteen days and I called Gina every chance I got and everything seemed fine. As time went on I was getting more and more excited to get done with this fire and go back home. At this point of the season everyone was pretty much over it and I wanted to go back and spend time with Gina. I kept counting down the days and soon it was time to head home. I was extra excited because I kind of figured this would be the last big fire of the season and I would start being able to go home more at night and I could start my off season with Gina. After a few hours of driving we stopped for some gas and I sent a text to her telling her we were on our way home. What usually was a response ending in an exclamation point and some excitement from her was now just, "Cool beans". That didn't sound right but I thought maybe she was busy or something.

We got back to the station, I gathered my stuff up and I drove home excited to have two days off and to see my girlfriend. I got home and called her and she soon came over. She sat down on my couch and looked like something was bothering her. I asked what was wrong and she basically hinted around that she didn't want to be together anymore. I asked her if that was what she wanted and she said yes. I was crushed. I didn't see it coming and had no idea what to say. I didn't say anything and soon she left. I just sat down on my couch and stared trying to figure out what I did wrong. I was crazy about her and she seemed to like me, but now it was over and I didn't know why. My first thought was I was gone too much and she found another guy. Then I thought about how maybe my weirdness had finally gotten to be too much for her. I thought about every possible reason I could think of and still came up with nothing. I was shocked. Everything seemed fine and she was always so sweet and cheery, but now she seemed like a totally different person. I called my mom and told her and she was shocked. They emailed each other every day and she had no idea Gina was planning on dumping me either. After I sat on my couch for a while and felt my heart break for the first time in my life, I went to a bar and had a few drinks by myself. I kept obsessing over why she dumped me. I just wanted to know why. If it was because she just didn't like me, then I wanted to know that.

The next day my uncle came over to visit me and walked in and said, "Hope I'm not interrupting you and Gina doin' it!" I just said no and didn't tell him that we had broken up. He's not exactly the person to tell serious stuff to because he will just make fun of you for it. I was happy to see him but I wasn't very talkative and I think he knew something was wrong. He left and the two days off I was so excited for, were now here but weren't so exciting anymore. I think I slept most of the first day and went and saw my dog the next. I was actually kind of looking forward to going back to work and going to a fire so I could keep my mind off of everything.

When I went back to work everyone kept commenting on how "ragged" I looked. I didn't tell anybody about it and just tried to do my work and move on. I certainly wasn't as motivated and of course we didn't go to any fires for a few weeks so I got to go home every night and think about it. I finally emailed her and told her I would leave her alone if she would just tell me why. She gave me a lot of reasons that I honestly didn't understand. A lot of little stuff that was never brought up and had it been, I could have tried to fix them. What I got out of the reasoning behind it all was I wasn't her type and she didn't like me enough. I replied to her email by simply saying I understood and goodbye. I asked her to drop some stuff of mine off on my patio and I too had left some of her stuff there along with some pictures of us and her. I didn't really want to get rid of them but I also didn't want to dwell on it forever and have to be reminded of how I had finally found a girl I liked but couldn't make her like me back the same way.

When I got home one day the stuff I had left for her was gone and my stuff was there waiting for me. I knew it was final now. It hurt to know it was over and I told myself I would never let myself get hurt like that again. Once again I had let my guard down enough to trust someone and allowed myself to open up to them and it turned around to bite me in the ass. Never again would I be so emotionally open to someone. I would go back to not showing any emotion and not let anyone or anything get to me again. I had to put that shield up again and protect myself because it wasn't worth it to let someone hurt me again.

There were only a couple of weeks left in the fire season and our Superintendent was in jail for a warrant, our captain left to go on another fire, our other captain quit, and we were missing three other guys, but still got called to go to Southern California for the big fires. We had to find replacements for all of those people before we could go the next day. We got a qualified guy from another crew to be our Superintendent, he brought three or four guys he knew, and our squad bosses wore the captains hats. Literally. They put on their red helmets and acted like they were the captains. Now we had all of that taken care of so off to San Diego we went.

That fire was an eye opener for me. It was totally different working for another Superintendent and it was so much better. It was more laid back and actually fun. We were allowed to laugh and talk while we were worked for the first time all season, and overall we were treated like adults for the first time. It was a nice change and got me thinking about how it would be on another crew and if I should apply somewhere else the following season. I never realized how miserable I was there under their regime until we had the new fill in boss. We worked hard only when we needed to and fought fire more efficiently and didn't have anyone standing over us barking at us to go faster. I think we actually ended up going faster and doing better work without all the barking. It was the first fire all year that I didn't hate being on.

Our last day of the fire was also our last day of the season and as soon as we got back home, we turned in our stuff and were done for the year. It was perfect. I really thought about trying to get on another crew for the next year but I still wanted to be part of this crew getting their hot shot status and that was supposed to happen at the beginning of next year, so I thought I would just tough it out and be treated like a child who couldn't think for himself for another year. It was getting really old being treated like that, but I needed the job.

We had an end of the year crew party and I went. Ordinarily I wouldn't have gone, but I had nothing else to do and I thought maybe I should start hanging out with people I work with. They had gotten us dinner at Boomtown, a hole in the wall casino, and had rented out a big room for us to drink in afterward. The dinner was all right and it was kind of fun until we went back to the room and started drinking. I remembered why I never went out with people I worked with now. People are totally different outside of work and it's kind of disappointing. The one's that are such good workers and seem to be level headed at work, turn into this out of control drinking and drug machine and are just ridiculous. They look like idiots and are more annoying than anything. It was obnoxious listening to them and watching them all night and I hung around as long as I could, but once the drugs came out, I left. I like drinking, but I'm not stupid enough to get into that.

The only good part of the night was I heard from Gina. I think I had sent her a drunk text or something and we went back and forth for a while. I didn't think we would get back together but it was good to hear from her and it gave me some hope. At least she liked me enough to text me.

The season was over, I was single and now I had nothing to do but sit around my apartment and rub lotion all over my naked body.

Some time went on and I emailed Gina every once in a while and finally asked her if she wanted to go have a drink sometime. She agreed and we met at some bar and it was awkward. I could tell she didn't want anything to do with me and I didn't really want to be just friends with her so I didn't get too excited. I think we might have met another time as well and I asked her if we would ever get back together and she said she didn't know. I figured it was time to move on now.

14

ONE OF MY friends invited me to go out with her and meet one of her friends and since it was pretty obvious Gina wasn't going to work out, I went and met her. I had gone to high school with both of them but didn't know them all that well and I felt very out of place. There was a group of people and I retreated back to my quiet self and as the night went on, I figured she wasn't interested in me. I got up and went to the bathroom and when I came back, the group of ten was now down to three, one couple and Leslie, the girl they were trying to set me up with. Now I was forced to talk and it ended up going better than I thought it would. We talked for a while and soon we were the only ones left out of the group, that couple had left. Things were going good so we decided to go somewhere else. We met up with some of her friends and kind of bar hopped the rest of the night until four in the morning. She was really cool and we flirted all night, but that was about it. I took her home and she told me to call her and we would go out again. This was the closest I ever was to "playing the field" in my life and it looked like my womanizer title might be reinstated. I was looking forward to going out with her again but it wasn't the same excitement as it was when I was going to go out with Gina again.

I was planning on going out with Leslie again but when Gina found out, she got kind of jealous and wanted to get back together with me. I thought that was weird that she didn't want to be together before but now that I was going out with someone else, she wanted to. I thought about it for a long time and went back and forth on it. I never, ever in a million years would have thought I was going to have girl problems and would have to "decide" (I guess) who to go out with. I knew if I went out with Leslie, I would probably lose any second chance I had with Gina. If I went back out with Gina, who knows if she would dump me again in a week or what. I didn't know what was going on in Gina's head but I had to go with my gut and my gut told me to try and make it work with her again. I never went out with Leslie again and slowly got back together with Gina.

I was happy being back with Gina but she never did seem to like me as much as she used to. There were a few times I thought it wasn't going to work out, but then the times we got along were so good, I wanted to make it work. It slowly got better and even though I still had my doubts about if she wanted to stay with me or not, I tried not to think about and wouldn't let myself get too worked up over it.

It was the beginning of a new year and I was hoping it would be a good one. It was not. My mom had recently gone to the doctor for her normal check up and they were having problems finding her blood pressure. They sent her to a vein specialist who told her she needed to get those little tube things called stents put in her veins and open them up. Sounded complicated and a pain in the butt, but if that's what she needed, then that's what she would do. It didn't sound too serious, so that was good at least. She then went to another doctor and they sent her to a kidney doctor. She called me that night after she got back from him and was crying and told me she had a form of kidney disease. She was very upset and very scared and I was as well. It was a shock, because she didn't have any of the symptoms and she seemed healthy and fine. She would find out more later but for now she had to get more tests done and just wait. After I hung up the phone I was scared for her and I cried. I didn't want anything to happen to my mama and I felt so helpless. I didn't know anything about kidney failure. I didn't know if she needed a transplant or if she just needed to be on medication or what. I called Gina and told her and I thought I was going to be tough enough to talk to her, but I got choked up and had to call her back. I felt like such a baby, but I was scared for my mom.

As time went on they told her she had polycystic kidney disease and needed a transplant. As if that wasn't scary enough, the doctors were of no help and told her she had to find out all of that transplant information herself and that the waiting list for a new kidney was about six to eight years and she would have to go on dialysis until then. That was terrifying to hear. Being hooked up to a machine for three hours at a time, four times a week is no way to live. We still found it weird that she didn't have any of the symptoms that go along with kidney disease. She continued going to doctors and getting tests done and had no idea what any of them were telling her because the doctors were more interested in sounding smart and building up their egos than actually explaining what is going on in normal person terms. Since my aunt was a nurse, my mom asked her to go along with her to her appointments and maybe ask questions and translate for her. Sounded like a good idea and made me feel better because I wouldn't have been any help.

My aunt very rarely asked any questions and didn't explain a damn thing to my mom. My aunt never showed any emotion her whole life and that's one thing, but if your family needs help, you help them, even if you are in denial about it all and selfishly don't want to get upset over it. She actually asked my mom to change one of her appointments so she wouldn't have to get up so early. My mom needed her to care and help her and she did neither. This was the beginning of the end of their once close relationship.

My mom started going to her appointments by herself and started getting some outside help on transplant information and soon was learning what she needed to do. My aunt was nothing but negative during all of this, telling her how transplants don't work very often and how she should just go on dialysis and how she was going about everything the wrong way. After my mom talked to the transplant people in San Francisco, she found out that just about everything my aunt had told my mom was wrong. There were no transplant hospitals or surgeons in Reno so my aunt really was in no way knowledgeable about it and even if she was, she should have been supportive for her sister, not negative and telling her there was no hope and she would be on dialysis forever. I'm not saying lie to people, but be supportive. A positive attitude goes a long way.

The next step was to try to find a kidney donor and the San Francisco doctors were going to be coming to Truckee and giving a class for kidney patients and would be taking blood samples from anyone my mom wanted to bring that was willing to give her a kidney. That was still a month or two away and I put in for that day off right away so I wouldn't be on a fire and miss it. When I went and asked if I could have that day off, my bosses looked at me and said no because we would be going through the hot shot tests right around then and they couldn't be missing anyone. I let them go on and on giving me shit for wanting a day off and then I told them I needed it off to see if I was a match to give my mom a kidney. That shut them up and I got the day off.

I could tell the upcoming fire season wouldn't be one of my favorites already and it hadn't even really started yet. We had our hot shot tests coming up and that is all anyone cared about. It was a whole different attitude and it was even more militaristic and controlling then before. The bosses wanted that hot shot status and they didn't care what got in the way. It was no fun at all. We had to clean everything a million times, reorganize our buggies a million times, go over the same shit a million times, and hear about how important this was a million times. They kept trying to intimidate us by telling us how picky and hard core the guys that would be watching us and testing us were going to be. It was going to be a two day event. The first day, these all important guys would come by and go over all the paperwork, test us on our knowledge of fire and our equipment, and inspect our station and our buggies. The next day, we were going to go out and cut line around a pretend fire and they would watch us and test us on different scenarios. All of that was supposed to happen in the beginning of July I think it was, so for the next few weeks, we worked our asses off and nothing was good enough. We got yelled at and criticized more than ever and none of us even wanted the hot shot status anymore. We were just there to go on fires and make as much money as we could and go home in the fall. To the bosses, this was life or death. They talked up being hot shots so much, I didn't even want to reach my little goal of being one anymore. It just didn't sound worth it anymore.

We had a week before our big test now and we had to go practice cutting line for the millionth time only this time was in front of one of the big guys that would be testing us. He was just going to watch us and get us ready for the real test the following week. No big deal, just do what we have always done, right? Wrong. Our bosses were out to prove something and we cut line like mad men. I started out at my normal pace cutting trees and brush and swinging the saw around and that wasn't fast enough. It had been fast enough the last two years but today I was told to go faster. So I did. I continued on for a while and was going along good but was sweating more than I usually do because I was going faster than normal and it was a humid day. I stopped a few times to get a drink of water and was told to stop stopping and I could drink water when we were done. I had no idea when that would be and I was really thirsty but I kept going. About a half hour later I felt really weird and weak. The sweat was running off of me and every inch of me was completely soaked. I tried to keep going but the saw was getting heavier and heavier and I finally had to say I needed to stop and get some water. I got some water and once the bosses came by and saw the big guy watching, they panicked and told me to get going again. I tried, but it didn't last long. I just couldn't do it anymore and the sweat was just too much. My mouth was so dry, my throat started to hurt and I was so thirsty I got kind of claustrophobic. They told me to sit down in the shade and I did, but I felt so thirsty and weak, I started to panic. My heart was beating a million times a minute and I couldn't catch my breath. I drank more water but it didn't seem to be doing anything and I kept panicking. I couldn't sit still and felt crowded even though I had plenty of space. The EMT on the crew came over and said I needed to get off the mountain but the bosses said no. I continued to sit there panicking and profusely sweating for a good half hour or so before I started to calm down. I was still so thirsty it hurt, but now I found it almost impossible to keep my eyes open. I was out of it. That's when they decided to take me to the hospital.

They called an ambulance to meet us at one of the nearby fire stations and we started driving out of the mountains. I could not keep my eyes open and the guy driving me had to keep yelling at me to stay awake. I have never felt so out of it before. We finally made it to the station and they had more people look at me and give me Gatorade and ice and eventually I felt a little better. It took the ambulance over an hour to get there and by the time they did, I was coherent enough to think it was stupid for me to go. My sweating had stopped and I wasn't panicking too much anymore but they still made me go. In the ambulance the paramedics gave me everything and tested everything. I think I fell asleep back there.

When I got to the hospital they gave me some more IV's and just diagnosed me with heat exhaustion and major dehydration. The doctor told me to drink more water and when I get hot, spray some water from the fire hose on me and to work without my hat on. He obviously didn't understand what I did. We were a hand crew, we didn't have fire hoses or a water supply. We were twenty guys out in the middle of nowhere with chain saws, Pulaskis, and shovels. That was it. I thanked him anyway and wearily walked out of the hospital because I still didn't feel very good.

During all of this, the crew got called to a fire and I had no idea where they were. I was dropped off at one of the fire stations with nothing but what I was wearing. We were a good two hours from Reno and even if I did make it there, I didn't have my wallet or keys to my truck or my apartment. I somehow found a ride to Truckee at least and spent the night in the barracks. The next day, I found a guy to take me to Reno, but still didn't have my wallet or any way to get into my apartment. I didn't care too much though, I just wanted to go home. I called Gina and asked her if she could pick me up outside of my place and let me stay with her until I could get my keys and stuff back.

When I got dropped off at my place I sat outside and felt like crap. I had a headache, was still thirsty, and didn't have the energy to walk. When Gina came to get me, she had bought me some clothes to wear until I could get into my place. That was so sweet and if I had felt better I would have been more appreciative. She took me to her place and I fell asleep with the air conditioning on. When I woke up I still felt like I was going to die but tried not to show it. Her parents came over and when they were leaving, I walked out with them to their car. As I was walking back, the heat of the blacktop in the parking lot got to me and I got all dizzy and felt like I was going to puke. I didn't go back outside for a few days.

I don't remember how, but somehow my keys and stuff were dropped off in Truckee and I was able to go pick them up and get back into my apartment. It had been a few days and I still did not feel good, but was better. My moms appointment was now only a day or two away, so I knew I was going to have that off at least. I figured I would go back to work after that.

My mom had her appointment in Truckee and had three of us that were willing to give her a kidney and we all went with her. It was me, Gina, and Gina's mom Whitney. My uncle had offered as well but he wasn't exactly the healthiest person in the world so I don't think that would have worked anyway. I don't think my aunt offered at all.

So the three of us drove up together and as we were walking towards the building, a car drives by us in the parking lot and this crazy lady with a crazy hat on, was leaning out the window rambling out all of this religious stuff to us. I don't remember exactly what she said, but our first reaction was she was just a crazy lady. We went inside and spent most of the morning there learning all about the transplant process, what my mom needed to do, etc.

It was sad to see how many people needed a kidney transplant and how sick they all looked. My mom still looked healthy and if nothing was wrong, but most of these people looked really sick. We then went in and had our blood drawn to get tested to see if any of us were a match. My mom got looked at by another doctor and then we went and had lunch in Truckee. We would find out in a week or so if any of us were a match.

A week or so went by and then one night as I was at home rubbing lotion all over my naked body, they called me and told me that I was a match. I thought great, lets rip my kidney out and give it to my mama. It was a very secretive process though. I didn't know if Gina and Whitney were matches too and my mom wasn't allowed to know anything yet. I was ready to get going on this whole thing as soon as possible and get it over with before my mom had to be on dialysis, so I just figured even if we all were matches, I would still do it. Then Whitney called me and told me she was a match as well and she wanted to do it. I felt weird about that, but Whitney is a stubborn lady and had a list of reasons why she should do it instead of me: kidney disease is supposedly hereditary so I might need mine later on in life; she only had a few more years of being able to give a kidney which meant if my mom ever needed another transplant twenty years from now or something, I would be able to do that; I needed to be able to take care of my mama after the surgery; she was older than me and knew more and to just not worry about it and let her do it. You can't argue with Whitney. You can try but it won't work. Although I felt weird having someone else go through the surgery and all of that instead of me, I had to agree. Whitney was going to donate her kidney and save my mom.

After some planning and organizing, just about everything was set. The surgery would be in September or October in San Francisco. My mom decided to not tell my aunt about it and I didn't see the need in telling her either, so she had no idea. As the months went on, she never asked what was going on with my mom or how things were going. She gave her a lot of info on dialysis and that was it. No questions, no supportive attitude, no interest, and just acted like nothing was wrong. That really got to my mom and didn't make the process any easier for her.

I soon went back to the crew. I still didn't feel like myself, but I thought I could at least manage. I planned on going back until the surgery, by then the season would almost be over anyway. The crew was on a fire and the boss had to come back to Truckee anyway, so I met up with him there and rode with him back to the fire. When we got there I just went back to work. I wasn't on the saw anymore and that was for the best because I still didn't have all of my strength back. I started out slow, but overall I did fine.

The next day we had to hike up a pretty steep hillside and it was easily a hundred degrees out. I used to be a pretty decent hiker but now it was really difficult for me to keep up. I kept falling further and further behind and the sweat was pouring off of me again. I started getting a migraine and had to stop. The next few days pretty much went the same. Just being out in the sun gave me a huge migraine and it was tough to keep up with everyone. I felt like I had aged twenty years overnight.

I made it through the rest of the time on the fire, although I didn't do much, and when we got back home, they said I should just try and take it easy when we go to another fire. We went home for our two days off and when we came back, we had a big come to Jesus meeting. We got lectured and yelled at for a good hour. A lot of people were having trouble keeping up the last few weeks and they didn't like that. Some were dehydrated, some were over worked, and some were just sick. The bosses were pissed and embarrassed and started letting people go because they were getting in the way of them becoming hot shots. They called a few guys into the office and when they came out, everyone looked pissed. They had let go of three people so far, some of them just for having a cold. Then they called me into the office. I already had a huge headache and I didn't want to sit there and listen to them lecture me, but instead of lecturing me, they let me go. They told me I was a liability for the crew and was having too much trouble keeping up. I was pissed because I was nothing but loyal to that crew the last two seasons and had always done a good job. I obviously wasn't feeling good because they wouldn't let me drink as much water as I needed and now it was my fault. I walked out and wandered around for a while. The more it sank in, the more I got pissed and the more overwhelming it got. I was once again out of a job, no other crew was going to hire me because of my condition, my mom was going through kidney failure, I couldn't go find some other job because I needed the time off to go to the surgery and then take care of my mom afterward, my rent was going up two hundred dollars a month and it all seemed to be hitting me all at once. I went and told them I was leaving and handed in my stuff. They told me to come back the next day to fill out some paperwork and do some stuff. They were still trying to control me even after I didn't work there anymore. I didn't show up the next day, fuck them.

That crew didn't get their hot shot status after all that. The big wigs who tested them said they were horrible and weren't ready for it. That day I went to the hospital, three other people went down as well. The bosses just didn't get it. They had blinders on and none of the people on the crew or their health mattered, it was all about building their ego and getting that status. The crew had a pretty bad track record. They had tried to get that status for years and never got it and every year someone got hurt. The first year I was there, some people blew out their knees and ankles from training too hard. The next season we had a guy go to the hospital because his kidneys were failing from dehydration and we had a girl cut her face with the chain saw because they were pushing her to cut faster to beat another crew.

Our crew was always out to prove something. We had to be the fastest hikers, even if it knocked out half the crew so much that we had no energy left to actually fight the fire. We were told to conserve our water, which is just plain stupid. Image was everything too. We had to all be wearing the same crew color even though it took them three months to get us our shirts and sweatshirts. So if we didn't have the right color sweatshirt on at fire camp, we had to do without and freeze. It was their job to supply us with the right uniforms, but we had to suffer because of it. It was just such an ego trip and it was ridiculous.

Although it sucked, I was glad I got the chance to get on a real crew and make some decent money and get the experience. I didn't ever want to go back to that crew again but I still wanted to keep fighting fire, mainly because it was all I knew how to do, but I wasn't sure if I would ever recover from my heat issues. That episode aged me a lot. I wasn't the same after that. I was constantly worried about it happening again and working out was a lot more difficult. I couldn't do things as easily as I was able to do before. It took months before I could run even a mile without feeling sick and getting a migraine. When I would hike, it was draining. I used to be able to just zoom up the mountain, but now my legs felt heavy and it would take me twice as long to make it to the top. The way I felt, I thought I would never fight fire again.

The next few months were both good and bad. Bad because I had no job and no income and my rent was soon going to go up, and good because I had a whole month of summer for the first time in a few years and I would get to do stuff with Gina. Things with her were going really good now and I thought it was going to work out even though I was still paranoid of being dumped at any time. My paranoia weakened though the more time I spent with her and it turned out to be a good thing that I lost my job and was around more. Had I been gone on fires that summer, we probably wouldn't have gotten back together.

Since it was going so much better, we talked about me moving in with her. We saw each other every night anyway and obviously it would help both of us financially and I figured this was one way to see if it was really going to work out or not. You never know someone until you live with them, so let's see if she still likes me after she really gets to know me. I knew I liked her enough and after all the homelessness, struggling, and the time sleeping in the woods for my job, I wasn't as difficult to live with. The stuff that used to be important wasn't anymore. I wasn't going to get upset if I had to wait for the bathroom or the cap wasn't put back on the toothpaste or anything like that.

I really liked my apartment and didn't want to have to move again, but I also wanted to live with her and it seemed like kind of a waste to have an apartment when I went over to her house every night anyway. I loved her, but I was hesitant to really let myself fall for her as much as I did before the breakup. I took a while to think about it and needed to make up my mind before my lease was up in about two months and I needed to stop over thinking it so much.

My mom and Whitney's surgery was now pushed back until December. I don't remember why, but it was frustrating to hear that. All of us just wanted to get it over with and to be able to move on and now we had to wait a couple of months more. It ended up being good though, I made up my mind and decided to take the plunge and move in with Gina. Now that the surgery was pushed back, I would have plenty of time to move my stuff before my lease ended and before the surgery. I moved most of my stuff into storage, again, and got all settled in her place the day before Thanksgiving, which was perfect because we would be going on vacation that weekend and then go to San Fran for the surgery right after we got back.

I really wasn't going to miss my old place that much. A lot of it had to do with me voluntarily moving for once and a lot of it had to do with there not being a whole lot of memories in that place. I spent the majority of my time there alone and was gone on fires for half the year, so it was just kind of a place to stay rather than a home. I also didn't think about missing it too much because I had more important things on my mind. I was nervous about it not working out with Gina, I was nervous about not being able to find a job for the next fire season, and I was really nervous about my mom and her surgery. I just wanted her and Whitney to make it through it all without anything going wrong at all. I was just too nervous to worry about missing my apartment.

Although losing my job sucked and I felt twenty years older now and was nauseous most of the time, it really worked out for the best. I was able to get back together with Gina and spend some good time with her and I was around to help with whatever I could with my mom. I couldn't do much, but I felt better just being around, just in case.

15

THE CLOSER THE surgery got, the more nervous we were all getting. Not nervous in necessarily a negative way, but more nervous of the unknown. None of us really knew anything about all of this and for me, it not only involved my mom, which is enough on it's own to make me a nervous wreck, but it also involved my girlfriends mom, which just about put me over the edge.

My mom finally told my aunt that she was getting a transplant a couple of days before it was going to happen. My aunts reaction wasn't excited or anything. I think all she said was, "Oh that's good" without a trace of emotion. Although my mom was nervous about the actual surgery, I think the fact that her sister didn't seem like she cared at all about her was tougher on her than the thought of going through the process of getting a new kidney. That upset her more than anything and made the whole ordeal a lot more difficult than it had to be.

I remember the day before we were set to leave for San Francisco. My mom had an appointment to get her hair done because she said if she was going to die on the operating table, she wanted to die with good hair. Her hair place was right near the Starbucks I went to and as I pulled up to it, I saw both my moms car and my aunts in the parking lot. I went over there and saw the two of them talking and I could feel the tension. My aunt didn't say much and gave my mom a couple of little gifts I think. She then said something like, "All right, let me know how everything goes" and then drove off. No good luck, no encouragement, no look of concern, and no hug. That pissed me off at how little she seemed to care. My mom was scared out of her mind at all of this happening and she needed her sister to be there emotionally for her but she was too selfish to show any emotion. I lost a lot of respect for my aunt that morning.

After my mom got her hair done, she came over to see me. She looked upset and told me how when she left the hair place, all the people there hugged her and wished her good luck and were nothing but nice and positive to her. She had strangers come up and hug her and her own damn sister couldn't even do that. My mom cried and I wanted to go tell my aunt off, but that wouldn't have helped anything and although it upset me, it was between my mom and her, not me. I told my mom we didn't need her anyway and everything was going to be all right.

The next morning we met at Whitney's house and my uncle was there to wish them both good luck and to give them a hug. That's what families do, they show up when you need them.

So my mom and I took her car and Whitney, Gina, and her dad took their car and we headed to San Francisco. It was about a three or four hour drive and when we got there we checked into our hotel and then had dinner and then went to sleep. The next day my mom and Whitney had to meet with a lot of different people throughout the day so we were on and off the shuttle bus and in and out of doctors offices a lot that day. She met with one doctor who told her he wasn't even sure she really had polycystic disease. When she told us that, I thought great, lets get back in the car and get back home! We then met with the surgeon and he was the most helpful and explained what was going on better than anyone else had so far, so that was a little more comforting. He told us how the numbers don't lie and no matter what disease she had, she still needed a new kidney. I learned more in that twenty minute meeting with him than the previous ten months of all the other doctors. He explained how the entire surgery would go, right down to how Whitney and my mom would be positioned on the table. I'm glad we got to meet with him because he made us feel better. He knew what he was talking about, not like all the other doctors who seemed like they were just guessing trying to make it look like they knew what they were talking about.

After all the meetings, I don't think we did much. My mom and Whitney rested in their rooms and Gina, her dad, and I went to the bar. My nerves were sky high and I needed a drink. We sat there for a while and tried to play it off that we weren't nervous and then went to bed pretty early because we had to be up at the butt crack of dawn the next day for the surgery.

We were then up before the sun and the hospital was nice enough to have a shuttle waiting for us. We went to the hospital, signed some papers and waited. We then went back to some rooms and my mom and Whitney changed into their gowns and the nurses took their blood pressure and all of that. We then sat there and waited some more. My mom hadn't eaten or drank anything in twenty four hours and she was starving. One of the nurses came in and asked me if I wanted anything to eat or drink and I said no because I didn't want to sit there and stuff my face in front of my mom, that would be rude. But the nurse kept rattling off all of the food and drinks I could have and the whole time my mom was listening to her and her mouth was watering. I kept saying I didn't want anything and the nurse kept naming foods like she was doing it to torture my mom. I felt bad, but it was kind of funny.

Then it was time for Whitney to go to the operating room. They had it all timed out so that as they took her kidney out, my mom would just be getting cut open and ready to have it hooked up to her without the kidney sitting around too long. Whitney got up and headed to the back and I wish I would have hugged her and thanked her but I didn't know if I was supposed to since the nurses were all leading her away. I wished I would have though.

After what seemed like forever, it was my moms turn to go back to the operating room. That's when the nerves hit me good. We walked back and they let me go into the little room just before the operating room. I got to put on a gown over my clothes and wear a hair net thing. We sat in the little room for a while and then it was time to go. We walked out and across a hall and then they said that was as far as I could go. My mom started to cry which made me cry and I hugged her and told her I loved her. I was so nervous and felt so helpless. I knew everything would be all right, both Whitney and my mom were pretty tough cookies, but it was surgery and that's not a relaxing activity or anything. They took my mom back and I headed downstairs to the waiting room to find Gina and her dad.

I took a while to get down there because I didn't want them to see me be a big baby, but I gathered myself up enough and found them. We then sat and waited. I know my mom and Whitney were getting cut open and all but I still think it was tougher on us just sitting there waiting. My little heart and my even littler brain were both racing. The hospital gave us pagers so that when the surgeons were done, they could page us and let us know how it all went. After a few hours we were really staring at those pagers. Then Gina's pager went off. Whitney was all done and everything with her went well and there weren't any problems and as soon as she got a room, we could go see her. That was a load off and it calmed me down some. Now I just had to wait for my mom.

Whitney was supposedly in her room now so we went up to see her. As we were headed to her room she was just getting wheeled in. She was out of it but looked good for the most part. She was just coming out from being under and we sat there and talked to her. I just wanted to squeeze her for going through all of this for my mom. There was just no way I would ever be able to thank her enough for what she had done. As we were sitting there, my pager went off. I headed down to meet the surgeon and when I got down there he was waiting for me and eating something so I knew it must have went well. He told me everything went absolutely perfect and I could see her in about an hour. I thanked him and shook his hand and then walked back to Whitney's room just smiling. So far everything had gone perfect.

It was now time to go see my mom so Gina and I went down to ICU to see her. When I first saw her she was zonked out with her mouth open. I went over and said hi and she just mumbled. I stared at her for a while and then it got a little too hectic down in ICU. People were rushing around and patients were bleeding and screaming and I just felt in the way. I decided to leave and come back later when my mom wasn't still under. She had made it through the surgery just fine and the nurses said she was already using her kidneys and peeing a lot, so I had nothing to worry about.

We went back to Whitney's room and I remember sitting there and looking at her and I got all teary eyed. I was so happy and grateful for what she did and was so happy they both made it through without any problems. I could finally relax a little and it had been an emotional day and I was now a big sissy and I didn't care. This was the first time in my life I had cried from being happy. I was exhausted though.

We let Whitney rest and went back to our hotel. I sat in the lobby and started calling people to let them know how it went. I called my uncle who was baby sitting my moms animals and told him the good news. He was very happy and relieved and I could tell he had been a nervous wreck all day. I then called my aunt. Unemotional as always, I couldn't tell if she was happy or not. I then called everyone on the list my mom wanted me to call. Everyone was so happy and relieved. Everyone but my aunt, couldn't tell with her. I know she is a nurse and has been trained to not show emotion, but come on, it's your family for crying out loud.

We then sat at the bar again. I really needed a drink now. We went back to the hospital one more time to check on them and then went to bed at like eight o'clock. It had been a big day.

The next day we went and checked on them and they were both looking a lot better. Whitney looked like nothing had happened to her at all and my mom was now able to talk. She was making a lot of pee and that was good, her new kidney had a lot of catching up to do. She was going to move out of ICU and up to her own room later on that day, so that was a good sign.

My phone had died the night before so I had to leave it in the room to charge for most of the day. When I went back to get it, I saw I had some messages. One was from my uncle wanting to know how it was going, and the other two were from my aunt wondering why I hadn't called her with an update yet. I was shocked because it actually sounded like she cared and was worried that something might have been wrong. I called my uncle and told him all was good I just didn't have my phone and he then called my aunt to let her know so I wouldn't have to deal with it. It was kind of nice to hear that she was worried though.

We spent most of that day checking on the girls and doing a little bit of sightseeing. The girls were good but were all doped up on pain killers so they slept most of the time, so we felt comfortable enough to go for a walk around San Francisco and the Wharf and get some of those little donuts with powdered sugar on them that they have down there. The day after that was pretty much the same only the girls were doing even better. My mom was now in a room and looked good. She had more color in her face and just looked healthier. Whitney looked like she was ready to go home and like nothing had happened.

It was now Monday and Whitney was being released from the hospital. It had only been three days since the surgery. That amazed me. We then found out my mom would be released the next day I think it was. I was even more amazed. How can you take an organ out of one persons body and put it in another persons body and have both of them go home three days later? They both looked like they were ready and I didn't question it, but I was amazed. They were released and we were going to drive back home right away but because of the weather, we had to stay an extra night.

We left the next morning and made it home with no issues. Whitney didn't need any help doing anything and my mom was a little more sore and needed help getting in and out of the car and such, but overall, was doing fantastic. We dropped Whitney off at her house, hugged her and thanked her, then I took my mom home.

I stayed at my moms for a few weeks taking care of her animals and helping her with everything. She had a lot of pills to take and it was confusing but we figured it out and she had some good days where she seemed more energetic than ever and some not so good days where her body was adjusting and she looked pretty puny. For the most part though, she looked a lot better than before the surgery. Not that she looked bad before, but now she looked healthier. It's amazing what a healthy kidney will do for a person.

After a few weeks my mom was able to do just about everything on her own and told me I no longer needed to stay there. I thought I should stay a little bit longer but she said she was fine, so I didn't argue. I packed up my stuff and although I had moved in with Gina about two months before, I still hadn't really stayed there yet between going on vacation, the surgery, and staying at my moms. I was really looking forward to it though.

My moms new kidney was named Floyd. Whitney had named her kidneys Floyd and Lloyd and had decided that she was giving away Floyd to my mom. I thought that was cute and I think it helped make everything go smooth. It was a positive attitude and helped make it more personal. There has never been any problems with Floyd. There has been no rejection, no sickness, no nothing, and every time my mom has her check up, they are amazed at how well she and Floyd are doing. They always ask her how many times she has been back to the hospital since the surgery. When she tells them never, they are shocked because it is almost never that good of a match and there is almost always some sort of rejection phase at the beginning. It was a perfect match and everything has been good since. Whitney is just like she was before, healthy and happy, and my mom is even better than before. Looking back, she did notice how her ankles were swollen and she didn't have as much energy before she got Floyd. It all worked out for the best and there is no way I could thank Whitney enough. She is both my mom's hero as well as mine.

I am in no way religious, but I still think that crazy lady with the crazy hat that drove by us and told us religious stuff when we went to have our blood tested had something to do with it all going so well. I believe everything happens for a reason and it wasn't just a coincidence that she drove by us at that exact moment.

I was now living with my girlfriend, something I never thought I would be able to say. Right from the beginning it was comfortable and we got along good. It was a comfy little place with just us and her two cats. I had grown up with dogs my whole life and had only known Arnold's cats for a short time, so it was all new to me getting to know the kitties. It didn't take long for me to love them and for them to tolerate me and I couldn't understand how some people aren't "cat people" because I think they are great. They are kind of like me, stubborn and independent.

My home life was now great, me and Gina were great, my mom and Whitney were doing great, so all that was left was a job. I had been working a little bit with my uncle but not enough to have a steady income so I figured I would give it a shot and apply with some more fire crews. I didn't think I would stand a chance after they knew I had my overheating issue, but I thought I would try anyway. I applied everywhere but really wanted to get on with a crew out of Carson City. They were one of the most respected hot shot crews in the country and I had always heard about how good they were. I put in my application on the website and a few days later, they called me. They asked me if I was still interested in the job and if I was, they would check my references and all of that. I said yes and then I waited. The next day I got a call from them asking me about my overheating episode. My old boss had told them about it and I thought I was screwed. I was honest and told them what happened and how I would not let it happen again and how I am out to prove myself again. They said they would continue calling people about me and let me know. After I hung up I thought there was no way in hell they would take a chance on me.

After some time went by, the boss called me and told me I was still in the running and if I wanted to, I could come by the office and meet him and ask any questions I might have. He made it sound very casual and like it was up to me if I wanted to show up or not, but I knew it was an interview. I went to meet him the next day and when I got there, I just sat in my truck for a while getting all nervous. Finally I couldn't take it anymore and went in to meet him and to plead my case. I went into his office and met him and we sat there and talked for a while. I explained what happened with me and what I was looking for and he explained how he ran his crew and what he was looking for. I asked some questions and it seemed like a much more organized crew than Truckee was and it sounded like they went on a lot more fires than Truckee did, which meant more money. After about twenty minutes, he told me he had two spots open on the crew and he would let me know but I was very high on his radar. I walked back to my truck and was pretty hopped up that I still had a chance.

As I was driving back to Reno, he called me and told me I was hired. It had only been about ten minutes since I left and I got the job! I was pretty excited to have another chance with such a good crew. He explained what I had to do and all the forms I had to fill out and it was still months before fire season started, but I knew I had a job now. It was a big relief and I was motivated to prove to myself that I could get back to the physical level I used to be and to be the hard worker I used to be.

So really, life was good now. I had a job to look forward to, I was living with my girlfriend, I had a nice place to live, and my mom was amazing the doctors every time she had a check up because she was doing so well. I was training as hard as I could to get in shape for fire season, but I was still a little hesitant on over doing it. I wasn't fully recovered yet but I was getting better and could at least run and sweat without getting a migraine anymore.

My first day on the crew was nerve wracking but pretty good. I didn't have any problems and I found out that I was going to be a sawyer. I really wasn't expecting that. I was a rookie on a well established, well respected hot shot crew and that usually meant I wouldn't be anywhere near a saw. I was just hoping I could handle it and wouldn't have any more heat issues.

My first fire season on the Black Mountain Hot Shot crew was a good one. It was a slow season but I still ended up making more than I did on Truckee and was treated a lot better. We could drink as much water as we wanted, were treated like adults, were allowed to talk and laugh while we worked, and didn't feel like we were being mind fucked all the time. There were no lectures everyday and when we went to a fire, we hiked up to it at a normal pace, did what we needed to do, then moved on. Everyone was there to fight fire and make money, not build up their ego and prove themselves to other crews.

During the year I heard a lot about Truckee and how bad they treated their people and how they were one of those "ego crews" who race up the mountain and over-do everything and end up just making themselves look ridiculous. I was so happy to hear that. I thought all crews were like that, but now that I was on a more mature crew, I saw how much better it could be. I wished I had been on this crew the three years before instead of on the Truckee crew. Truckee eventually did get their hot shot status that year though, after years of trying. Good for them.

I made it through the season with only one minor heat issue. I was being paranoid and caught it before it got bad and everyone understood that and it was no big deal. I still wasn't fully recovered, but for the most part, I did better than I expected and I had a good year being a sawyer on a hot shot crew. I guess I had finally reached my goal. Rather anti-climatic. Not too big of an accomplishment for most, but for me it was nice to see what reaching a goal felt like.

My second season on the crew was a lot better than my first. I had a little more confidence and didn't have that "new guy" tag over my head and I actually came out of my shell a little bit. As time went on, I felt more comfortable being myself and started to feel even better physically. Not as good as I was before the over heating issue, but slowly getting back there. A few months in, I started working on my Firefighter 1 task book which just meant I got to start carrying a radio instead of a saw and have more responsibility and began to "be in charge", or at least be a training "in charge guy" under direct supervision. Doing that helped me come out of my shell even more and I really started to like having more responsibilities and being on my own more. It was nice to be the guy leading instead of the guy following for a change.

The season went on and it was a lot busier than the previous season. I wasn't at home much and worried about Gina and how she was handling it, but she said she was fine and couldn't wait for the end of the season so we could go on trips. The more I was gone though, the more I wanted this to be my last season so I could spend more time with her. I liked the money, but I liked being home and being with her more. I was debating for the first few months whether or not I would go to an engine the next season so I could be home more and then one night while I was at home with Gina eating dinner, my phone rang. They told me I had to be at work in the morning and we were going to a fire somewhere in Utah. I hung up and looked at Gina and she was all teary eyed and told me how much she hated this. I felt so bad. I never wanted my job to be my life and that was exactly what it had become. I told her it would only be a few more months and I would be free and I wouldn't be doing this the next season. I meant it too. Money is nice, but the people you love are more important and you shouldn't sacrifice relationships with them for a few extra bucks.

September came and we were again on another fire in Utah. This one was going pretty good and we were busy everyday and we were out of cell phone range so I couldn't call home to check on my mom or Gina but we were only supposed to be there for a week or so since we had been working for the last week on another fire. After a few days, we had been moving around the fire a lot and got somewhere where we had cell coverage so I called Gina. She was very short with me but I just thought it was because she was out to dinner with her nail lady. I let her go and then called my mom. She had to take Lewis to the vet because he had been throwing up but it sounded like everything was going to be all right and the vet commented on how good he looks for his age. After I hung up, I found out we were going to go to a different area of the fire and camp out up there which meant we probably wouldn't have cell coverage. That sucked because I wanted to be able to call and see how Lewis was in a few days.

The few days went by and we only had two days left before we got to go home. Then we found out we had gotten extended for four more days I think it was. That was morale killer. At this point of the season everyone is sick of it and just wants to get it over with. I was upset because I knew Gina would be upset and I had no way of calling her to tell her I wouldn't be home when I said I would. I also wanted to hear about Lewis and what was wrong with him.

The next day we got more good news-we were extended another three days. Everyone freaked out and searched for a place to be able to make a call and eventually they found one. I asked to use one of the guys phone and called Gina. I left a message telling her what day I would be home and told her to tell my mom. She called back and the guys phone was almost dead so I had to make it quick. I asked how everything was and she was again short with me and sounded different. She then asked me if I had talked to my mom. I said no. She said I needed to. I told her how I only have about a minute left on the phone and then she told me that Lewis had died. I was crushed. I thought everything was going to be all right with him. I didn't know what to say and she kept asking me why I was sounding so weird. I snapped at her and told her how I just found out my dog had died, what do you expect. I hung up and tried to keep it together because I was around people and people are assholes and probably wouldn't understand why I was crushed about losing my best little buddy and just would have made fun of me. I held it all in like I have been accustomed to all of my life and that was difficult. Instead of breaking down, I got pissed. I was pissed that this stupid job kept me from being there and had kept me from seeing him or my mom for the last two months and had kept from seeing Gina for a month. At least I figured out why she had been so short with me.

I have loved every dog I have ever had, but Lewis was one of a kind. He was like my little brother and he pretty much ran the family. I loved that little guy so much and I knew the day would come, but that doesn't make it any easier. He was a family member and anyone who thinks that's stupid and he was just a pet, can suck my ass. I like animals more than people. They are run by their instinct, making them honest and loyal no matter what. People are run by their ego, making them dishonest and disloyal. People have never earned my trust, animals have. As long as animals keep liking me, I know I am doing something right.

We ended up going back into camp where there was phone service and I kept trying to call my mom but she never answered and never called me back. I knew she was crushed and didn't want to talk about it, but I wanted to know what happened and if she was at least sorta all right. I never got to talk to her so I called Gina. Something was up with her. I thought it was just because she didn't know how to break the news to me, but now it seemed like more. It wasn't the same Gina. A lot like when she broke up with me before—awkward conversation and she very rarely returned my texts, both of which were very unusual.

After twenty five straight days of work, we finally got to go home. I was excited because this was probably going to be the last fire of the season and we would just have one more trip to Vegas to do some project work and then that would be it. But the excitement was dulled a lot by constantly thinking about Lewis and worrying about my mom and Gina. I still had not heard from my mom and the texts from Gina seemed forced. Even though I found it hard to believe, I told some of the guys that I bet I would get dumped when I got home. I had been living with that constant paranoia for the last two years, since she dumped me out of the blue for no good reason. Couldn't really happen though, right? Just two weeks ago everything seemed fine, she was all excited for me to be back home and was planning a trip for the first weekend I was off after the season. She had also just bought tickets to the Raider game on my birthday and had planned another trip for later on in the spring too and it was only a few weeks ago we were talking about getting a house together and she had always dropped hints about getting married. How could that have changed in two weeks?

After a ten hour drive of being stuck in my own head, I was finally home. I had a funny feeling when I got to the front door, but I just figured I was over thinking things. Gina gave me a kiss hello and I kind of felt relieved for a second until I saw the look in her eyes. She was cooking dinner and looked different. I asked what was wrong and she said nothing. I asked again and she said we should talk about it over dinner. I told her no, just tell me now. She said she had not been happy and asked me if was. I told her I was and she just gave me a condescending look. I told her there was only one thing that I wasn't happy with and if we could just work on that, everything would be great. She didn't see things the same way and said how she didn't want to make this bitter. That was it. I knew it was over and my stomach dropped. I didn't know what to say. I had been working for the last month straight, my dog just died, and I'm not even home ten minutes and I am being dumped and it just dawned on me that I have to find a new place to live now. I only had two days off before I had to go back to work and go to Vegas for two weeks, how the hell was I going to find a place and move all my shit in that time? She very lovingly told me that I could keep my stuff there until I was done with work. Wow, really? How nice of you! You really do care about me! Thanks a bunch!

I went and took a shower since I had no idea where I would be staying that night and started to get more pissed. I couldn't believe how heartless she was and how much of a stranger she was all of a sudden. I didn't even do anything wrong, I had just been working. It's not like I cheated on her or anything. I thought everything had been fine and now all of a sudden I find out she hasn't been happy with me for the last year? I had been lied to all this time and that pisses me off more than anything.

I felt so stupid. She couldn't have mentioned once how she wasn't happy in the last year? She couldn't have said something to try and fix it instead of lying to me and pretending everything was all right and then all of sudden quit? And not that there is ever a good time to dump someone, but really? Now? She really must not have liked me at all.

I got out of the shower, got some stuff I would need for the night, and took off. I wanted to go off and scream at her, but I have gotten pretty used to controlling my temper. I really should have though, because it is still eating away at me a few months later.

I stayed at a casino that night and sat at the bar and just couldn't believe it. My life had just been turned upside down. Four days ago I had just found out my favorite dog in the world had died and then I finally get to come home from work after a month and have a couple of days off and I find out I have been dumped and need to find a new place to live but can't really look for anything yet because I have to be out of town for two weeks. At least my truck didn't break down.

I finally talked to my mom and asked her if I could stay at her place. She said yes of course and my two relaxing days off were spent moving as much stuff as I could into my storage. I moved quite a bit because I wanted to get it over with as quickly as possible. After a day of moving as much as I could, all I got was a text from Gina saying, "Wow, you were busy today!", like she was proud of me helping her out or something. She didn't even seem to be sad at all. The next day I moved more and got frustrated that I didn't have a place to put everything and got more frustrated that I couldn't get it all out of her way quicker. It's a horrible feeling to be somewhere you are not wanted.

That night I was at my moms and I went and checked my Facebook just to see if she wrote anything to me or about me. It had only been a day and she already put a post up that she was single. That hurt. Facebook is stupid and I don't really care about that, but the fact that she showed no respect, no emotion, and made it seem like she just could not wait to get rid of me in the blink of an eye after almost four years, hurt me a lot.

I went back to work and when everyone asked how my weekend was, I told them. They thought I was joking at first. When they realized I wasn't, they were very supportive because they understood how heartless it was of her to do that all of a sudden at such an inconvenient time. Made me feel better, because I thought I was just being too sensitive and making too much out of it, but when everyone else was just as shocked as I was, I felt like it was ok to be upset.

We left for Vegas and although it was frustrating to have to be away instead of looking for a new place and moving all of my stuff, it was kind of good to get my mind off of it for a while. The first few days I couldn't concentrate very well, but then it got better. The last day there, my stress started coming back though. I had so much to do the second I was laid off for the season and I was having trouble shutting my mind off and didn't sleep very much.

The season ended and what only a month ago seemed celebratory was now a stress filled pain in the ass. I had to find a place that I could move into as quickly as possible, move my motorbike out of *her* storage before I could move *her* stuff that was in *my* storage into that storage, and I couldn't move any of my big stuff out of *her* place until I had a place to move it to because I had no more room left in *my* storage. I found an apartment pretty easily but could not move into it for another two weeks and that was driving me crazy. I hated not being able to just get all my crap out of her way and be done with it. I didn't care how long it would take for me to get settled in to my place, I just wanted to get out of her place. She seemed like she couldn't wait for me to get out and I hated waiting around while all my stuff was just sitting there in her way.

Finally I moved into my apartment and the last thing I had to move from her place was my aquarium. It's quite the project to do that alone, but I had moved everything else by myself, couldn't stop then. I did that with no problems, then said goodbye to the cats, looked around and got choked up, locked the door and left. I sent Gina a text asking her where she wanted me to leave her key and she replied by telling me not to worry about it and to take good care of the fish. It seemed like she could not have been happier to get me out, and that this was no big deal. I guess for her it wasn't, she had obviously been thinking about this for a long time and she wasn't the one that had to start her life all over again.

It's been a few months now and it's still eating away at me. I've been trying to move on but my confidence is shot. It took me thirty years to get a girlfriend and she dumped me twice in the three and a half years we were together for no specific reason, which only means she didn't like me enough.

The loneliness has been overwhelming. I have been used to being around twenty people at work for six months straight, spending twenty four hours a day with them for weeks at a time. I have been used to being around Gina every other moment I'm not at work for the last three years and texting and talking to her on the phone when we couldn't see each other. Now it has all stopped. I have no one to talk to all day, no one to text, no one to go eat with and all I do is sit in my apartment alone and try to get motivated to draw, which seems impossible most of the time because the silence and depression paralyze me.

I'm new to this relationship and breaking up thing and it seems so weird to me how it has to be. You spend years with someone and they are your everything. You tell them everything, you go everywhere together, your decisions are made with both of you in mind, you constantly think about them and look forward to seeing them every moment you are not with them, and people stop recognizing you as an individual and start only seeing you as half of the partnership. They are your whole world and then it just stops. They have become a sudden stranger. The partnership ends for whatever reason, sometimes no reason at all, and that's it. No more calls, no more talking, no more sense of humor, no more even seeing them. It goes from one extreme to the other in a second. I don't get it. Just move on I guess.

Now that I am single, I'm planning on going back to Black Mountain next fire season and have been working out even harder to get in better shape and get past all of my heat issues. I don't just want to be in good enough shape anymore, I want to be one of the fastest and strongest on the crew. I want to make it through a season without any tiredness or weakness getting in the way. It gets harder the older I get though. My knees are constantly hurting and that has really slowed me down a lot and has made hiking a lot more difficult. I just have to work harder at the gym which sucks because I hate the gym. I love working out and all that, but I hate the gym scene. There are way too many douche bags at the gym. I call them "gym bags". They are the ones that act like they are professional athletes because they were physically talented enough to buy a gym membership and have a wristband around their forearm. They have their little workout outfit and half a bottle of cologne on and a full bottle of protein shake with them. They are constantly looking at themselves in the mirror and if they aren't flexing and posing, they are at least puffing up. They act like they are in the best shape out of anyone there even though you never see them working out their legs or running any faster than a slow jog because if they went any faster they wouldn't be able to flex their pecs as much. They are the ones that tell everyone how they go to the gym for three hours a day but that's only because they do one set of curls and then go walk around all puffed up for fifteen minutes before they do another one. *They are there* for three hours but they have only done about ten minutes of exercise total. And the tough guy looks are enough to make me want to vomit. I am not impressed that you bench pressed three hundred pounds two times. You are not a bad ass because you grunt and scream while doing a set of squats and I think you are an idiot for dropping those dumbbells after you do curls. These people obviously need the big muscles and the special hair cut though because they need some way to get people to notice them, their personalities sure won't get them noticed.

So yeah, I need to go to the gym more. I couldn't care less what my physique looks like, but I want to be able to outwork everyone. Like I said, I plan on staying on Black Mountain until something else comes along and who knows how long that will be. I know I don't want to do this for the rest of my life, but I still have no idea what it is I want to do. I don't necessarily see that as bad thing anymore though.

There are advantages and disadvantages to being on a hot shot crew and that's why I always have to decide if I am going to keep going back every year or not. On the positive side, I only work six months out of the year and make enough to not have to work the other six months. It's really nice to have that freedom all winter. I not only make decent money in those six months, but I also get to save a bunch of it. While I am on a fire, I don't spend a dime for two weeks. I don't have to buy gas or food and everything is taken care of. I also get to travel a lot. Even if it's only to different forests that are on fire, it is still pretty cool to see everything in between and we get payed to sit and enjoy the ride. Firefighting is one of the most respected jobs there is and it's nice to shut people up like "gym bags" when they find out I do that for a living. It's one of the toughest jobs out there and I like that. Another advantage is that there is always light at the end of the tunnel. It's not your basic nine to five job where all you have to look forward to is a vacation a few weeks a year. I have a short attention span, I need something to look forward to and an end to strive for. I look forward to the end of the two weeks on a fire, getting to go home and relax for two days, the end of the season, and I even look forward to getting in shape for the next season. I like that my year is non-monotonous.

The disadvantages make every year want to be my last. I have no life in the summer. I'm only home about two days a month and I miss out on all the summer activities. I miss the Fourth of July, I miss spending time at my moms and her big backyard full of flowers and coziness, and I miss my two favorite events of all time; the Rib Cook Off and Street Vibrations. I don't get to ride my motorbike very much at all. It only has 6000 miles on it in five years. I want nothing more than to just ride it and enjoy the summer. Another disadvantage is that it is such hard work that it is taking it's toll on me and my knees. When I come home from a fire, all I want to do is sleep and not be outside in the heat. My knees hurt so bad that going up and down stairs makes it look like I'm ninety years old, and going up and down mountains all the time makes it feel like they are just going to snap.

The biggest disadvantage is the time I miss with my family. I never wanted my job to become my life and that is exactly what it has become. I am on call all summer so I can't be more than two hours away anytime, I am gone for two weeks at a time and sometimes without phone service, and I never know where I will be the next day. I never really get to see my mom, uncle, or my home. I get home and then two days later, I'm gone again. I worry about my mom being alone and not being able to be there if she needs anything and not being able to help my uncle if he needs it. It all just seems to be too much for a job I don't love. I like it, but I don't love it and if you're not passionate about what you're doing, then you should find something else. Unfortunately I have fallen into the trap of sticking with a job I don't love because it is all I know and can't afford to start over doing something else.

I don't know what that something else would be anyway. I can't see me doing any one thing for the rest of my life. I have had eighteen jobs, give or take a few random day jobs, and I wouldn't be surprised if I have eighteen more in my next thirty five years. I wouldn't change anything from those eighteen though, I have learned a lot from them all. Mostly I have learned what not to do, but more importantly, I have learned that I still have a lot of learning to do.

I would like to try and make a living by drawing, painting, or writing. Something where I get to be creative and do what I want without being "supervised" by someone. If I could just do that and work by myself, for myself, that would be as perfect as it could get for me I think. If I had it to do all over again I would do that or work with animals in some way. Either a veterinarian or trainer or something like that. Animals and art are the only two things I am passionate about I guess.

No matter what I do, I will never take a job too seriously and let it effect me or my life. I always try and keep the two separate. I don't get wrapped up in the gossip, the backstabbing, or the questioning of how things are run. I don't take it personally and don't get upset if I have to do more work than someone else because they are too lazy. It will just make me look better when all is said and done. I will work my butt off, but I am there for a paycheck and that is all. I don't want my work life to be my social life, I don't want to think about work when I am at home, and I don't want to be known for what I do. I do it strictly for the money so I can eat, live under a roof, have some stuff, and go places.

I have never had many friends and I still don't. Actually I don't have any friends. I still talk to Arnold a couple of times a year at the most, but that is it. We just have different lives now and don't have as much in common anymore. I'm a mountain man and he's an actor. I carry a chain saw around a burning forest, he wears make up and pretends to be someone else. Neither one is better than the other, but it's hard to relate to each other anymore because we have such opposite lives now. I have known him for twenty five years now and he is my only true friend and I wish we were still as close as we once were, but it's tough when we live in different states and have such different lives. He has been successful so far at acting and I hope he becomes even more successful. I don't know what his plans are and what he wants to get out of acting, but I really hope he makes it and is happy. He has helped me a lot in my life and I am grateful for that and I hope someday I will be able to repay him.

Other than Arnold though, I have no friends. I don't keep in touch with anyone from high school or L.A. I like the guys on the crew but I never see them outside of work. I don't have one guy I could call to go out for a beer or anything. It sounds sad, but not really. I'm shy and awkward around most people anyway so it's kind of better to just keep to myself. I don't understand the people that always need to be around other people and be in contact with them. With all the Facebook and Twitter crap that is going on, it seems like people are afraid of being by themselves for more than a minute. I don't get that. If you can't be comfortable by yourself and you constantly need to be around other people or know what everyone else is doing, that's just not healthy. There is a difference between being lonely and alone, I don't know if people realize that.

Overall, my family is doing pretty good. My aunt is still clueless about how she treats people and why my mom doesn't talk to her anymore. She is getting older and I think all the years of being reserved are taking a toll on her. She is still negative and critical when she talks about people, but then justifies it by buying them things. I don't talk to her much anymore and the nice guy in me feels bad about that, but then I think about how she treated my mom and how she talked to me when I was little and it's hard for me to get over that.

My uncle is very unhappily married but just deals with it. He spent years complaining about her and being miserable, but instead of leaving her he has just accepted it as how it is and that's that. He must not be as miserable as he has lead us to believe. When he was first having issues with his wife though, he went to therapy and I thought that was great. He ended up only going for a few weeks though and then got upset because he wanted answers and they weren't giving him any. I guess a lot of people think like that. They want the therapist to fix them and that's not what it's about. I have been a depressed wreck for a lot of my life and I have figured out that it is all in my head. It's all perception and no one can give you an answer that will change your whole life around just like that. The point of a therapist is to help you change your way of thinking and they need time to get to know you and see how you think before they can start to change it and they can't just come right out and tell you that's what they are doing or you will try to control your thinking and you won't be as honest and then that doesn't help you at all. It has taken your whole life to think like you do, you can't just change your thought process overnight.

My mom and Floyd are healthier than ever and so is Whitney. Both me and my mom are still friends with Whitney even though her daughter is now a stranger to me. My mom has tried to remain friends with Gina, but I don't know if Gina has put much effort into doing the same. I hope she figures herself out someday.

My mom was very lucky to find a donor so quickly and have it be such a perfect match. I am forever grateful to Whitney for doing all of that and I was really hoping that my mom and her would hang out after they recovered. I worry about my mom being lonely and I don't want her to end up like me, not wanting to go out with anyone because it's just too awkward and uncomfortable. The comfort of just staying home and avoiding change is an easy trap to fall into and I don't want her to do that. She's not happy and that makes me unhappy. She works her ass off and is treated like crap, gets no help, and is expected to make her work her life. She is doing really well and is successful and is very respected, but she didn't go through all the crap she has been through in her life to make her work her life. She didn't get Floyd to just go to work and then go home and be too tired and grumpy to want to do anything else and I wish there was something I could do to get her out of that job and out of that funk. She needs something else in her life other than work and that is why I was hoping her and Whitney would be really close after the surgery. My mom needs a good friend and I think they would both make each other happier and be good for each other. I just want her to be happy.

I just want all of my family to be happy. That is all I wish for. I only want everyone to live a long healthy life without anything bad happening to them. I will take on whatever I have to as long as they will be ok. I would keep working until the day I die if it meant my family wouldn't have to.

If I had enough money, I would pack up my mama, my uncle, my aunt, and move them all to somewhere tropical and none of them would have to work. They could all do whatever they wanted to do. My mom could ride horses on the beach all day, my uncle could ride motorcycles all day, my aunt could do whatever it is she does, and I could just draw and write. That's all I want. I don't think that is too much to ask.

16

I STILL HAVE NO idea what it is I want to do with my life and I am still not successful. I have never really succeeded at anything. My only successes have been overcoming my failures. But I don't think it is too late for me because at least I have learned why I have failed so much. I used to spend all of my energy just trying not to fail, instead of trying to succeed. There is a big difference and it all starts with attitude. My attitude had me stuck in my past and I used that as an excuse. I have figured out that my past has absolutely nothing to do with what I am doing now or what I will be doing.

I have been through a lot. I was kidnapped, beaten and belittled by a man who I didn't know was my dad. That was only one of two times I have ever seen him. I was molested. I was homeless for almost a year. I have been so broke I thought I was going to starve to death. I have lost the ability to trust because of men like the dentist who used to bruise my chest to get me to stop moving, my Pop Warner coach who got put away for life for being a pedophile, Russ for being a pedophile, and my dad for being an all around asshole. I have spent the majority of my life so lonely it hurts and feeling alienated around everyone and feeling out of place everywhere I go. I was only 'with' one girl, one time, the entire decade of my twenties. That took more of a toll on my mind that I had ever thought it would.

But through all of that, I have never taken drugs, am not an alcoholic, never been arrested, didn't give up, and have no desire to harm others the way they have harmed me. That might be my greatest accomplishment. I could have very easily given up on life, continued to be trapped in my past, and just taken the easy way out and lived my life only to feed an addiction, but I never did that and I think that is more respectable than overcoming an addiction. I'm tired of hearing about celebrities and sports stars overcoming addictions and how strong and brave they are. That is bullshit. The real strong and brave ones are never weak enough to get addicted in the first place. I don't care what anybody says, addiction is all in your mind and you can control it, you just have to be willing to control it. There were a lot of times I wanted to drink until I couldn't feel feelings anymore, but I knew better. I knew that would be weak and I would just be giving up. I was strong enough and self aware enough to catch myself and not let myself be that stupid. I don't want anyone to ooh and aah over me, I was close to losing it, but I think oohing and aahing for someone who was stupid and weak enough to get addicted in the first place isn't as ooh-worthy as the people that stay strong no matter what.

I'm not as much of a wreck as I used to be since I figured out I didn't have to be and it wasn't helping anything. I'm secure enough to admit I'm insecure and I make fun of myself for it. I don't take myself so seriously anymore and I have taught myself to not be in denial about anything. Some people don't understand my self deprecating humor. After years of being criticized for everything and anything, I found it is easier to criticize myself first, before anyone else had the opportunity to. If I beat them to it, they almost never agreed with me and turned to a compliment instead. It's just a lot easier to hear myself making fun of myself instead of hearing someone else do it.

I don't have many preferences anymore, I'm just happy to be here. I don't care what kind of food I eat, as long as it fills me up. I don't care where I go or what I do on vacation, I'm just glad to be able to go anywhere but where I am. It's not that I don't care, it's just that I don't have any preferences. I'm seriously happy just being here and being alive. I don't get mad very much at all anymore. I don't get too excited either. I don't take anything for granted. I don't get stressed out over things I have no control over. I don't get stressed out over things I do have control over because I know I should just change them if I don't like it. It's basically a lot easier to live a life for the big picture, not for all the little crap that gets in the way.

I still have days where I feel depression knocking on the door trying to get in though. It's been hitting a lot lately because of Lewis and Gina but usually it's rarely about something in particular. Sometimes I just wake up and am bummed out. People don't get that. They always ask me what am I depressed about and that's when I know they don't get it. It's not always about something. Sometimes it just goes back to how I have been alone so much that I just want to be quiet. Sometimes things just aren't funny for no reason. They might have been the day before, but now, not so much. Sometimes I am just both physically and emotionally tired. I have worked hard and have used up a lot of emotions already in my life, it catches up to me every once in a while.

And sometimes I just wake up thinking about my regrets. I know that isn't healthy or productive, but sometimes I just can't stop thinking about how much time I wasted being stupid and I can't help but think about how my life would have turned out if I had the same attitude and work ethic back in high school that I do now. I wish I would have tried harder at playing football so maybe I could have played in college. I regret not getting into firefighting earlier. I would have grown up quicker and had a lot more money and probably would be in a higher position by now. I wish I would have tried to become an actor, the curiosity of that will always be on my mind. I wish I could have been a normal guy in his twenties and sowed his oats, if you know what I mean(although that wasn't entirely up to me because I couldn't make someone like me).

And sometimes I get bummed out just thinking about the good old days and how simple it was then and how overcomplicated it is now. I miss being a little kid and carefree. I miss our family Christmas'. I miss looking forward to coming home after school and playing men and playing with the dogs in the backyard. I miss playing Pop Warner football and seeing my mom and Gran in the crowd. I miss the rides home with my mom after she picked me up from Grans. I miss playing in the front yard with Arnold and getting excited about baseball cards. I miss my childhood. When I was young, I wanted nothing more than to grow up and be on my own and now that I am on my own, I want nothing more than to go back and regain my childhood.

I am in no way religious. I think believing there is a man up in heaven watching us to see if we are being good or bad is just a grown ups version of believing in Santa Claus. I have never hit the snooze button. I don't like tomatoes. I have learned to never get too excited or too low because it will always turn around. Chicken wings, seafood, and chocolate are my favorite foods. Not together though. I think about L.A. everyday. I'm in favor of gay marriages and abortion. It's none of our business what other people do, if it doesn't effect you, stay the hell out of it. I think ninety five percent of Oscar nominated movies are the most boring movies ever. I think technology is making us dumber and lazier and is over complicating everything. I have been sexually frustrated since puberty. I have noticed people have a different attitude when they chew gum. I don't like The Beatles, The Doors, Elvis or Jay Z. I think people that have had a "normal" childhood are more screwed up than the rest of us. I wish people would use their blinkers. I think farts are funny. I don't think stereotyping is. I'm only racist against assholes. I don't trust people with mustaches, especially women. I have never been fishing. I think I'm funny looking. I don't respect anyone I haven't met. I am very sexually inexperienced. I think there is too much importance placed on fashion and hair. I have never met a dog I haven't liked. I can't say that about people. I think social networking is stupid. I have never shot a gun. I am not a morning person. I think if more people did some form of physical activity everyday and didn't take themselves so seriously, there would be a lot less stress in the world. I don't care who you are or what you do, there is always someone who can do it better, so don't be cocky. I don't understand how our country is in economic turmoil, but we can donate millions and millions to another country after a disaster. I think we should be able to donate millions and millions to people in our own country that are having their own medical disaster and can't afford health care. I think people talk too much and don't listen enough. I have never learned anything by talking. I think too many people are in a hurry to do stuff that really isn't important. I think people should stop comparing themselves to everyone else so much and concentrate on trying to make themselves better than they were the day before. I believe everything happens for a reason even if it takes your entire life to figure out why.

So there you go Todd, I told you about myself, go ahead and take the "little bit" out of it that you want."

Todd just looks at me with that fake interested look on his face and I can't tell if he is smart enough to know that I came to this interview just to waste his time and to vent or if he thinks I am really answering the question and want the job. The blank look on his face could go either way and then he uncomfortably looks at my application again and asks me, "So, why did you apply here and show up for the interview if you already have a good job you are going back to soon?"

I'm kind of shocked he asked me that, I was expecting him to ask me where I saw myself in five years and continue on with the interview.

I respond, "Because I have had it with the whole interview process. From the desperation, to the nerves, to the awkward conversations, to the leading me on only to never hear from them again, to the douche bag managers. You managers make me sick. You are all the same. You are arrogant, fake, and completely out of touch with reality. You are more concerned with selling yourself as something you aren't and using these interviews as a little stage to show off your over enthusiastic fake personality and to feed your ego, rather than to learn about the person you are interviewing. I have spent years being frustrated going through this process and now that I don't have to anymore and hopefully will never have to again, I am going back to some of the places that I have interviewed with in the past that I have never gotten out of my head. I remember interviewing here when I desperately needed a job and was talked down to and strung along for weeks before I found out I wasn't hired. You completely wasted my time and made me feel like an idiot for jumping through your hoops which only helped feed your superiority complex. You kept me hanging on only to benefit you and now I have kept you hanging on and wasted your time to benefit myself. I needed to do this. Not only for the resentment I have towards all of this, but also for my own well being. I have spent my life being misunderstood and have never really been able to just vent and give some of my opinions before. Anytime I have tried, I have either been made fun of, criticized for being too serious and stupid, or it has just been too uncomfortable for me to talk to anyone I know about serious things, so I'm unloading it all onto you.

So to answer your question, I came in here to mock you, make you as uncomfortable as you have made me, waste your time like you have wasted mine, and to get some things off of my chest and vent to someone I have no respect for and will never see again. I have no desire to work here, I don't care what you think of me, and I think you are trying way too hard to be something you are not. You look and act ridiculous and I think you are a complete tool."

Todd just sits there looking at me in disbelief as I stand up and walk out of his office without saying another word. As I walk out towards the front door I look over and see the girl in Capri's staring at me. She looks like she just stepped in shit and I just wave at her and tell her to have a nice day. She half heartily waves back and I walk out feeling better even though I know I still have a lot of unresolved issues.

I stop by the coffee place on the way out to my car and buy a four dollar cup of coffee and don't even think twice about it. I sit there and drink it and people-watch for a while and think about how lucky I am to be able to do this.

I finish my coffee and walk the half mile back to my car. I get in and check my phone and see that I have a new voice mail. I wonder if it's Todd! I call my voice mail, enter my password, then press pound. It's Bryce, the manager at Claim Jumper asking me to come in for an interview tomorrow. I hang up and start remembering how nervous and desperate I was for a job when I interviewed there about six years ago and how they treated me and lied to me and told me how much they liked me but still never gave me a chance. I start reciting my spontaneous answers to all of the standard interview questions I'm sure I will be asked and drive back home still feeling very fortunate that I have a home and a job.

I sure hope Bryce doesn't ask me to tell him a little bit about myself, I never know how to answer that.